TALE OF AN OLD, BOLD PILOT

JIM SHOUSE

iUniverse, Inc.
Bloomington

Tale of An Old, Bold Pilot

iUniverse books may be ordered through booksellers or by contacting:

iUniverse
1663 Liberty Drive
Bloomington, IN 47403
www.iuniverse.com
1-800-Authors (1-800-288-4677)

Because of the dynamic nature of the Internet, any Web addresses or links contained in this book may have changed since publication and may no longer be valid. The views expressed in this work are solely those of the author and do not necessarily reflect the views of the publisher, and the publisher hereby disclaims any responsibility for them.

Any people depicted in stock imagery provided by Thinkstock are models, and such images are being used for illustrative purposes only.

Certain stock imagery © Thinkstock.

ISBN: 978-1-4502-8739-5 (sc)
ISBN: 978-1-4502-8740-1 (ebook)

Printed in the United States of America

iUniverse rev. date: 2/10/2011

Contents

FOREWORD   vii

CHAPTER I A HIGHLY IMPROBABLE DREAM   1

CHAPTER II ENTERING MILITARY LIFE   8

CHAPTER III MAGELLEN THE NAVIGATOR   12

CHAPTER IV FINALLY THE FRONT SEAT   18

CHAPTER V FLYING THE LINE   28

CHAPTER VI LEARNING HOW TO CHANGE A FUSE   33

CHAPTER VII UNDER THE AURORA BOREALIS   36

CHAPTER VIII SCHOOLBOY ONCE MORE   42

CHAPTER IX ELECTRONIC MARVELS   46

CHAPTER X COMBAT   57

CHAPTER XI WORLDWIDE FLYING   66

CHAPTER XII WRAP UP OF A CAREER   79

CHAPTER XIII WORKING FOR A LIVING   89

CHAPTER XIV THE ABUNDANT LIFE   93

EPILOGUE   100

FOREWORD

This is an account of a young man who was fortunate enough to get to perform a job that he desired a great deal. How few people ever get such an opportunity! Many start a journey in a specific direction yet, somehow they become diverted somewhere along the way, and their direction changes. So many, many things can and do, occur to alter their direction and efforts that few ever reach the goal that they set for themselves. How sad!

The young man in this story had a dream at an early age, kept jealously to himself, lest he be laughed at by his brothers, his family and friends. He pursued those directions that he learned from several sources after he started formal education. There was very little to encourage him in his locale, and he was forced to search through libraries and written materials for information that would help him reach his goal. Some of the information gleaned from these resources was not at all correct; however, it did not sidetrack or dissuade him from his quest!

If there is a thrust or purpose to this book, it would most certainly be to encourage young people to set a goal for the major aims in their lives and to pursue that goal doggedly. One must allow room for disappointments, setbacks and interruptions without departing from the desired goal. Keep on keeping on! Roll with the punches; do not be easily discouraged or dismayed. Expect resistance to well planned activities, and always keep in mind that a thing of value has a price tag attached to it. Believe me in most cases, the item desired will be well worth the cost. A wonderful sense of accomplishment will also be attained, self-confidence will be gained, and fear of failure will be cast aside. Always press on to the goal that has been set!

This young man desperately wanted to become a pilot. He was versed in Lindbergh's writings along with several other authors who detailed their experiences and somewhat glamorized the art of aviation. There is an old adage that states: "There are old pilots and there are bold pilots, but there are very few old bold pilots." This account is aimed at taking issue with this old adage, and relating the experience of an old, bold aviator who has lived through enough to write about.

His experience may seem boring to some, while others may relate to them thorough their own trials, experiences, failures and successes. Whatever one's experience, he should keep in mind, from the beginning of this book, that the young man of this story lived the events herein; they are factual and true. This is not a novel or fiction in any way. It is my hope that the reader of this account will set his or her own goals with little doubt that they can actually be reached, attained and enjoyed. PRESS ON!

CHAPTER I
A HIGHLY IMPROBABLE DREAM

At the age of four years, a noise caused me to look up nto the sky, in the back woods of Northeastern Mississippi. Much to my surprise, I saw a thing with two wings and a motor that was imitating a bird and staying well above the trees. To my question, "What is that thing?" I was told it was an airplane. Well, during this period of my life, it was a big treat to see a bicycle or a car, but an airplane was beyond my knowledge of vehicles. My curiosity was, indeed peaked, and immediately, my desire to learn more about this phenomenon began earnestly.

At the age of four, my education was somewhat limited to only a few experiences. During the Great Depression, as this story begins, I was familiar with two saw mills, powered by steam, that my father operated with his six sons, and ran a farm also. We were reared to believe that one only gets what one earns. Nothing of value is free!

Up to this time, a brother of mine had introduced me to the intriguing taste of peach brandy as we walked along a path to his house, where I was to spend the night with him and his wife. My parents were low key but strict disciplinarians; fair in every way and constant teachers of what is right and good, and they would have descended on my brother like a "Hen on a June Bug" had they been aware of his actions.

The first grade in school was well-worth waiting for. This was the start of my quest to learn about that mechanical bird that I had seen. Discipline was strict in those days. It was easy for me, for it was what I already had learned at home. For some kids, it appeared harsh and disagreeable. One young man, dressed in green short pants with shirt to match, held up his hand and asked to be excused so that he might visit the rest room. His request was quickly denied without explanation. The young guy sat there for a few minutes and then began to bounce his legs up and down. This action increased until finally, I noticed that he was crying. As the tears rolled down his face, water began to drip and run down from his seat. He was urinating all over himself! Naturally, we boys began to snicker, the girls blushed and finally the teacher noticed and quickly took him to the principal's office. His mother was contacted, came and took him home.

Later, at the time of Thanksgiving, the school put on a review, honoring the season. I was in my first review and public performance, and was riding a wave that was unfamiliar to me. After the program, I stood with my mother awaiting the arrival of my brother who was driving our open-topped sedan made by Chevrolet. He quickly swung the car around, ran up a sloped bank and then came flying backward, showing off his automobile handling prowess. Before he got into reverse and came flying backward, I decided to get a jump on getting a choice seat, so I ran behind the car in an attempt to go around it. Guess what? Yep! The car came back faster than my legs carried me. It hit me, knocked me down, and proceeded on over me. I still remember the hot oil dripping into my face as they pulled me out from under the engine. Needless to say I was bruised, skinned, and sore all over; yet, there were no broken bones. Wonderful!

One might say that there are many indicators pointing to the probability that I must be accident-prone. I don't think so; it seems that the more activities in which we are involved increases the chances for accidents and injuries. When I was nine years old, my older brother and I loaded a truck with firewood for the upcoming winter. This truck had no cab on it, and the bed was open for ease of loading and unloading. We completed the loading and jumped up on the seat. My brother tried to start the engine while going lickety-split down through the woods. He couldn't get the truck in gear, and told me to jump. I stood up to jump just as we hit a tree. I went flying off onto the ground, and the wood found its way all over me. Again contusions, bruises, skinned places, but no broken bones.

Just about that time, even though I had lived in the country and was highly familiar with forests and such, I still had not learned how to swim. One day my brother and sister, along with other friends, and I went for a swim in the lake. The sloping bottom quickly pulled me well into water over my head. Since I couldn't swim, I went under, saw many bubbles around me and decided that this was the time I was going to die. I felt something and grabbed at it. It was my sister who also couldn't swim, and I almost caused her to drown. My brother rescued me and a lifeguard saved my sister. When I regained consciousness I was lying on the ground coughing and gasping for breath. You know, flying can't be any more dangerous than this! The next year, I learned to swim.

My friend and I organized a Boy Scout troop in our hometown, and really went for scouting in a big way. On one occasion, we hiked up, Lebanon Mountain, which was the largest hill or mountain in our part of the state. We camped out in our pup tent and bedded down for the night. Unknown to us, this particular night the foxhounds were running in our local area. We heard a sound like someone walking around outside our small tent. My buddy turned and opened the tent flap a small amount, and found that he was staring directly into the eyes and nose of a large foxhound! Our tent became a bit disorganized, and almost collapsed as we both were trying to get away from that big bear, or so we thought!

During the sixth grade, it came my turn to give an oral book report. At this point, I must say that in our part of the state, we had our own dialect, and spoke with a very flat pitch. If we intended to say fire, it would sound like FAR! My report was on Jack London's, *"Call of the Wild."* I neared the last part of the story and intended to say, "They sat down and started a far." In my haste to finish before the final bell, I said, "They sat down and farted a star." At my age, this was the most embarrassing event in my life! The boys all fell out of their seats, rolling and hee hawing on the floor, the girls all blushed immensely and looked the other way, and the Lady Teacher tried to regain her composure and her own control without laughing. Suddenly, the bell rang, saved me, and I rushed from the room as fast as my legs would carry me. I'm sure that my face was three shades of red!

It seemed as if I was always getting into trouble during my High School years. One day, while sitting in the "Study Hall" reading, I was hit in the eye with a Lima Bean that some wise guy shot with a rubber band. Naturally, I let out a yell; for it did hurt quite a bit! I was summoned into the Principal's Office along with the "SHOOTER", and since I also had a rubber band in my pocket, even though I was innocent and had not shot any, I got the same paddling as the shooter. We both got it! Then on another occasion, I put a small piece of paper down a friend's collar. I was seen by the Principal who summoned me to the front of the Study Hall and paddled me sharply in front of the whole room. He never was one of my favorite teachers! Guess I must have been a pill, for I learned later that the Principal lost his mind!

While a junior in High School, I rode with four guys in a new pickup truck to a basketball game a few miles down the road. The driver started to pass a vehicle, when up popped a car coming straight at us. He swerved, lost control of the pickup and down off the highway and into a large ditch as we rolled over and over! I received a large lump on my forehead, but continued on to the game, played in it, and it was one of my better performances.

About this time, my friend and I went to a pasture in a town nearby and got our first ride in an airplane. It was an Aeronica Champion, a high-wing cub-type aircraft. The flight was much too short for my liking, for I loved every minute of the flight. This whetted my desire to learn how to fly and continued my quest for more information about flying.

Although, I was a student who studied and obeyed the teachers to the letter of the law, I still was disliked by many of the boys in my class. As a senior, my first class teacher in the morning would call me up to her desk, ask for my homework, then hand me the keys to her car and say, "Go drive my two daughters to school in a nearby town." That was a snap! I did my work, and graduated first in my class in four years of High School.

While I read everything that I could find in our library concerning aviation, I did attempt to study mathematics, physics, and chemistry and have my transcript reflect such. After High School, I attended a Community College in Booneville, Mississippi, where I also graduated. Somewhere I had read that aviators had to be exceptional in math and physics. This really isn't true, but in Community College, I studied Pre-engineering. The hardest math a pilot encounters is division, learned in grade school.

In the area where I grew up, annual revivals were on the slate of most churches. Baptisms were usually performed in a nearby stream that had swimming holes deep enough for immersion. On one such occasion, an older fellow in the neighborhood was baptized. This particular old fellow was notorious for constantly swearing and cursing. A few days after his baptism, the old fellow was teased by his co-workers and questioned if he really did get baptized. His reply broke them up as he said, "Hell, yes, I did! That damn water was cold as hell!" My area of the country seemed to produce a breed apart.

During High School and Community College, I was active in basketball, baseball and football. Football was added to my sports activities in Community College. We had no football at the High School that I attended, and I attended my first year of Community College on a basketball scholarship. An altercation with the Center on our team ended my basketball scholarship. The following year, I tried out for the football team even though, I had never been in a football uniform. Much to my surprise, I earned a scholarship for my second year.

Toward the end of this second year, The USAF sent a recruiting team to our school for the Aviation Cadet Training Program. About twenty of us guys decided to apply and take the one-week long testing at Moody AFB, Georgia. Only two of the group passed the exams and were offered an entrance into the Cadet Program. I was fortunate to be one of the two who passed. Upon review of the test scores, I was told that I had passed for Observer Training, which included such positions as Navigator, Bombardier, Radar Intercept Operator, Performance Engineer and several other flying jobs. I was informed that I did not pass for Pilot Training. Since the Draft System and the U.S. Army were breathing down my neck, the Observer Training did include flying, so Observer Training, here I come!

CHAPTER II
ENTERING MILITARY LIFE

I was sworn into the United States Air Force at Jackson, Mississippi, and promptly flown to Lackland Air Force Base at San Antonio, Texas. What a shock this was! I began to wonder if a flying job was worth all the trouble it took to get one. Aviation Cadet Training is a very rigorous experience for any young man. Eating a meal while sitting at attention was an experience very difficult to describe. Upper Classmen, those who were one month and two months more experienced than us Third Classmen would call us by name, and we had to respond within three seconds or be given demerits. We were only allowed a set number of demerits each week. If we exceeded this amount, we had to walk on the "tour path" one hour in dress uniform on weekends, for each demerit over our limit. This part of Cadet Training was called "Pre-flight Training".

We had classes where we were taught many things about the Military in general and the Air Force in particular. We marched everywhere in Flight and Squadron Formations. We were hazed constantly by the Upper Classmen who made us march single file around a sidewalk square, three times before entering the barracks, giving commands to ourselves. What fun! Also, the "Uppers" would stop us and demand to know, "Mister, what are you famous for?" We had to think fast and reply with something as stupid as, "For being a glow worm, Sir!" At which the "Upper" would reply, "How so?" Our response would be something as inane as, "When I gotta glow, I gotta glow!" Originality was expected, and if the "Upper" was not pleased, we got a 'gig', which was short for a demerit. Different offenses carried different penalties; for instance, one offense might produce twelve demerits, seventy-two hours on the tour path and three months restriction to the barracks! That happened to one of my roommates, and yet he did graduate.

After Pre-flight Training, I was transferred to Harlingen AFB, Texas that is located near Brownsville, Texas, the southern most city in Texas. This phase of training was considered Primary Training and included the primary elements of flight training in non-pilot positions. Each Saturday, we were graded by inspection of our persons, and our rooms, with white gloves. These inspections were tough to pass, and each squadron was graded against other squadrons. The one with the lowest score was called the "Eight-ball Squadron", and had to take PT, physical training, or calisthenics before breakfast for a week.

At Harlingen AFB, especially in winter, the place was home to a great many Grackles, which is a large black bird very similar to a Crow. One particular morning, my squadron was dubbed "Eight Ball", and I had the dubious 'honor' of directing and leading the P.T. As we were involved in an exercise called the 'side-straddle hop', some Grackles flew overhead and bombed one of our students. The student quickly requested permission to fall out of formation since his flight suit was well decorated by one particular bird. His request, of course, was denied and the next exercise was push-ups. I told him, "Stay in there!" A lot of laughs ensued at this point, and all heard some very colorful language.

While in training at Harlingen AFB, we were given instruction in the effects of altitude, known as 'Hypoxia' (a lack of oxygen and its effects), and the ability to recognize our own indications while at altitude. We were required to enter a pressure chamber wherein the air was gradually removed so as to simulate certain levels of altitude. We were told to remove our oxygen masks at 25,000 feet and work with the man sitting next to us. This way, we learned our own indicators of Hypoxia, and readily watched as our partner passed out from lack of oxygen. He was not aware that he was unconscious, so we then hooked up his oxygen supply. It was both interesting and comical when the oxygen got to him, for his limbs began to thrash about involuntarily. Also, as the chamber climbed to 43,000 feet, the gas trapped within our bodies began to expand enormously. The belly and abdomen both began to swell, and we quickly began to rub our bellies from right to left. If the gas was not eliminated, pain became sharp, until it was removed. There was danger of rupturing an intestine or the colon. It was perfectly natural to see several young cadets rubbing their mid-riffs vigorously until a smile came upon their faces! Since there was so much noise in the chamber, we heard nothing or smelled nothing. However, before we were allowed to exit the altitude chamber, all the air was removed and the chamber refilled with fresh air. Most of the guys exited with smiles on their faces.

Our training missions were flown in T-29 type aircraft. This is a twin-engine propeller driven aircraft, and we received training in all phases and types of navigation in them, from Day and Night Celestial to Pressure Pattern,

Radio, and Radar, Loran and other types of visual and Dead Reckoning. This was a very good, dependable and safe aircraft. In September 1954, I was married to a young lady with whom, I attended church, and approximately two months later, I graduated from Observer/Navigator Training School. I had already received my commission as a Second Lieutenant in August, some thirteen months following my enlistment. I was then transferred to MacDill AFB, Florida, as a Navigator who had won his wings.

CHAPTER III
MAGELLEN THE NAVIGATOR

Upon arrival at MacDill AFB, Florida, I was assigned to an aerial Tanker Squadron, as a tanker navigator on KC-97G aircraft. My job was to maintain a proper position of the aircraft in respect to the mission for that particular flight, and also to control Airborne Rendezvous Procedures with bomber and fighter aircraft, refuel them in flight and send them on their way toward their targets. The Rendezvous Procedure was to direct my aircraft, and oft times a flight of five tankers to a particular point and take up orbiting at that position. Then I was contacted by a flight of, usually five jet bombers, and started to talk them into position to rendezvous with the tanker flight. The bombers were usually at thirty-odd thousand feet altitude, and we tankers were at about fifteen thousand feet. I started the bombers descent so as to arrive at our altitude about two miles behind us, while also giving them heading changes and corrections to find us without having to make huge time-consuming turns.

As a general rule, the bomber leader usually took my directions without question or comment. However, on one occasion over the Atlantic Ocean, I could hear the leader of the bomber flight tell his flight to go in the opposite direction from my instructions. For instance, I would give a heading to the leader of fifteen degrees right. A few seconds later, I heard him tell his flight, fifteen degrees left. I knew that his navigator was reading my beacon incorrectly and the flight would miss us by taking his navigator's corrections. I requested my Aircraft Commander to allow me to turn off my beacon, and I explained why. He refused me permission, and the Bomber Flight missed us by at least ten miles. This required them to make a huge 360-degree turn, in formation, and delayed their refueling to a dangerous point. Thereafter, when I requested something from my Aircraft Commander, he promptly gave it.

On my first trip across the Atlantic Ocean, my Aircraft Commander had never flown with me that far, and he seemed a bit nervous. He asked one of my friends if I would get him lost out over the Atlantic. My friend replied that I was an Instructor Navigator and was steady as a rock. During the long flight, my AC would walk by my navigation table, stop and ask me, "Where are we?" I immediately put my finger down on the flight plan and said, "Right here!" He would say, "Good!" We probably were not within a hundred miles of the point where I had placed my finger, but he didn't know that, and it kept him happy! On this flight, to Lajes Air Base in the Azores Islands, off the coast of Portugal, while inbound to Lajes, I gave him a final heading and an estimated time of arrival over the field. When that ETA expired, we were right over the Air Base at Lajes. He never questioned my headings or ETAs again. I might add, this Aircraft Commander had been recalled during the Korean War, and was a trumpet player for Les Brown's Orchestra. He was a terrific Aircraft Commander and a good pilot.

I spent four years at MacDill AFB, and spent temporary duty in the Azores Islands, Ben Guerir AB, Morocco, Tripoli, Libya and several Air Bases in England. While visiting in Libya, in fact, within the city of Tripoli, my buddy and I went sightseeing with a guide. We noticed that along the streets, many old men in their robes, were sitting just off the street. Most of them appeared to have only one good eye, for the other was white throughout and they looked to be blind. I asked the Guide why this was the case, and what caused so many men to be blind in one eye. He replied, "The blindness is caused by flies." What a lesson on the lack of cleanliness, hygiene and common sense. One temporary duty stint gave me my first opportunity to visit London, England, and experience the lovely weather there. On one trip to Libya, we noticed a foreign fighter aircraft on our left wing. He was close enough for us to see the pilot blink his eyes, and his oxygen mask moved up and down as he talked to someone, probably his home base. We thought that he came from Tunisia. He made no indications that we were to follow him, so we just continued on our way. Near the end of my tour at Mac Dill AFB, I was required to check my records at Wing Headquarters. There, in those records, I found my original scores for pilot school, and learned that I had passed them; the Air Force needed navigators and observers at that time. I retook the exams once more, and had no trouble in passing with a good score. While awaiting a class assignment for pilot school, some Aircraft Commanders even gave me some "stick time" in the tankers. Terrific!

While stationed at MacDill, my first child, my son, Eric, was born in a hospital in Tampa. My wife was in labor for thirty hours, and finally the doctor forced the birth. Otherwise, everything was normal, and we were blessed.

Also, during this tour in Tampa, I was fortunate to hear a famous colored preacher named, Marshall Keeble, preach at Temple Terrace College. That was, indeed, a treat, for he was a very polished and gifted speaker. One particular comment that he made still sticks in my mind. It was a response that he made to a question posed by someone in the audience, concerning his view of biblical commentaries. He said, "It is amazing how much light the BIBLE sheds on commentaries!!!"

My time as a navigator, approximately four years, was extremely valuable to me later, when I entered pilot training. For instance, with about twelve hundred hours or more in the air, I found myself unconsciously orienting myself on every flight. It was something over which I gave little thought; it just happened automatically. Feeling comfortable in flight was adopted early.

On my first trip to Ben Guirer, French Morocco, a great deal of detailed planning became absolutely necessary. As we squadron navigators were planning and preparing our charts for the long trip, I noticed that s friend of mine was preparing only one chart for the entire trip. A pencil mark could easily cover five or more miles and the scale of the map was not good for actual flying, but only for course planning. I pointed this out to him, but he refused to listen, and attempted the complete ocean crossing with the inappropriate map. Needless to say, he could not readily know the position of his aircraft, his Aircraft Commander declared an emergency, stating that he was lost and running low on fuel. However, he did manage to reach his destination and land safely. While at this forward base, I had to fly with my friend and confirm the information passed by him to the Aircraft Commander on his next flight to England. He finally learned to utilize the correct maps for all future flights. He ended his flight career as an airline pilot.

Occasionally, we were required to fly over high northern latitudes utilizing polar navigation procedures. This is where the magnetic compass is unreliable because of the location of Magnetic North. There is quite a distance between Magnetic North and the True North Pole! While flying under Polar Procedures, a Directional Gyro is rated for precession, and used instead of a magnetic compass by which the aircraft is steered. As an aside, usually speaking, the crew navigator is looked down upon by the two pilots as a sub-standard crew officer. However, if the navigator wants to gain either pilot's attention, all he has to do is stand up from his navigation table, throw down his divider or pencil and loudly proclaim, "Oh, Crap!" Immediately, thereafter, the pilots treat him like a king, since he is the only one who knows their accurate position or they hope that he does! For the remainder of the flight, he gets everything that he wants, unquestioned! They do not want him lost or confused.

On long flights, our Naviguesser, as he is affectionately called, utilizes drift readings, pressure pattern, day celestial, using the Sun and Moon, night celestial using stars and planets, Loran, radio bearings, tacan stations, VOR (Variable Omni Range) bearings, dead reckoning and Consol. He keeps the pilot advised with reference to course corrections and estimated time of arrival (ETA) at points along the flight path and at destination. He keeps the Radio Operator apprised of positions for reports that he must make. The Boom Operator is also advised of the Receivers' (Bombers or Fighters) positions and ETA for the "refueling envelope". The navigator on a tanker aircraft is a key and valuable crewmember. He is the source of information for all the other crewmembers.

I did receive extremely valuable experience in a multi-engine aircraft as a crew navigator that helped season me early in my career. Military flight training by the USAF is, by far, the absolute best in the world. No other country or training school can come close to USAF training.

I heard one navigator say to another, "I can go anywhere since I learned how to navigate. But, I did get a puncture in a tire one day, because I didn't see the fork in the road."

CHAPTER IV
FINALLY THE FRONT SEAT

After approximately four years and some twelve hundred (1200) hours of flying time, as an Observer/Navigator, the USAF finally allowed me to leave the Tanker Squadron and my navigational duties and enter into Primary Pilot Training.

I was transferred to Bartow Air Base, Florida. My entry into this training was what I had long sought and desired most in military service. After having to wait so long, just to enter training, and spending nearly five years in a non-pilot job, I fully determined that I would not wash out of training easily, but would fight, tooth and nail, to satisfactorily complete this, my only opportunity to reach my goal.

We moved to Winter Haven, Florida, got used to a new and different house, and prepared for our second child. At Bartow AB, our instructors were all civilian pilots, trained by the Air Force, and very good at their jobs. My instructor, Mr. Al Lincoln, whom we referred to as Abe, was wonderfully gifted as an instructor. He was even-tempered and astute at vocal as well as actual demonstration of flight maneuvers and procedures. Formal classes were also necessary in order to prepare us for flight instruction.

The first plane that we flew was a single-engine propeller driven aircraft built by Beechcraft, and known to us as a T-34. This low wing, tandem cockpit aircraft was our first attempt at flying and was our first in which to solo. The first solo in flight training is extremely important, and the first rung on the ladder of self-confidence, which is a must if we are to be successful in the school. My big day came unexpectedly as we pulled off onto the parking apron, and I prepared to shut the engine down. My instructor quickly advised me that he was getting out, and it was my turn to make a fool of myself. He got out of the rear seat and closed the canopy, gave me a thumbs up signal and headed for the parking lot.

I received taxi clearance from the tower, and ran my pre-takeoff checklist. I was finally cleared for take-off for my first supervised solo. (We were required to fly three supervised solos where our instructor went into a small control unit near the runway and both watched the flight and monitored the radio chatter.) As I made my takeoff roll, the plane seemed to jump into the air, since the rear seat was empty.

As I started my climb to traffic pattern altitude, I thought, this is a breeze! Little did I know what lay just in front of me! But after flying the traffic pattern, I turned in on final approach, and started staring at the end of the runway. The aircraft seemed sluggish and my airspeed started falling off. Finally, I realized that I was getting 'low and slow'; the 'kiss of death', and yelled into the radio, "I'm going around". Later, I was told that the tower had told me at least twice to "go around", but I did not hear for my hands were full at the time.

I came around the pattern again and on final approach, I had to use all of my self-discipline to even look at the runway. Somehow, this time, my airspeed was good, and I heard, and felt, the landing gear chirp on the concrete. I opened the throttle, said out loud, "This is a piece of cake", and promptly took off again. We had to make three 'touch and go' landings on the supervised solos, and this was the greatest self-confidence builder that I had ever experienced. I never had a problem from that point on, for I was convinced that I could do this job of piloting this little bird. I had to log thirty hours in the aircraft prior to moving on to the next aircraft which was a T-28, single engine low wing monoplane, but much more powerful than the T-34.

This second aircraft was also easy to learn to control both on the ground and in the air. Both of these first two aircraft were equipped with tri-cycle landing gear. That means that they have a nose wheel and two main landing gear wheels. Aircraft with tail wheels are difficult to control while on the ground.

A friend of mine, with whom I carpooled, and I decided to cancel our membership in the Officers' Club. We were working and studying sixteen hours per day and only rested on weekends; when we spent time with our families. Immediately, after terminating our membership, we were called before a military officer, a major, one of only thirty military personnel who were stationed there. I was told that I was weak morally, anti-social, and did not take the opportunity to associate with my brother officers! He also said that he would give me the lowest military grade that he could. WOW! My friend and I went back and rejoined the Officers' Club and paid our dues. Since only thirty military personnel were permanently assigned to that field, it appears that those officers feared that we would start a trend among the students, and so many would drop their club membership that the club would have to close!

I passed this on to my civilian instructor, and he passed it around to our classmates. A long story short; my friend and I received the highest military grades in the whole class!

As our training was continued in a higher-powered aircraft, the radial engine powered T-28, flying became much more fun. We had lost several students in the first aircraft who were unable to solo the plane safely. In this heavier bird, we were introduced to "instrument flying", and we performed this in the rear seat with a hood made of canvas that came up from behind us, went over our heads and snapped to the top of the instrument panel in front. This was designed to prevent our peeking out to see if we were right-side up or whatever position we were in. Our instructor told us the following story about one of his students.

It seems that this particular student was caught several times by the instructor as he peeked and tried to ascertain his correct position rather than by his instruments. So one day, the instructor knew that he was peeking, so he quietly unhooked his seat belt and harness, turned around in his seat so that he was facing the student, quickly raised the front of the student's hood and said very loudly, "I told you to stop peeking and fly by those gauges!" It really got the student's attention, and he never peeked again. In this phase of our training, we had to log one hundred hours flying time in the T-28 aircraft prior to moving on to Basic Training at a different base.

My next assignment was at Laredo AFB, Texas, with training in the single engine jet. This training included formation flying, instrument and contact flying while learning to fly as a fighter pilot. It was at this base that my second child, a daughter who we named Anne, was born. What a delightful little girl came into our family. This phase of my training was devoted to flying a single engine jet and developing along the lines of a fighter pilot. Three other guys and I were assigned to an instructor, Lt. Allen MeNair, and we used the call sign, "Maverick".

One of our indoctrinations in this school involved a ride in an ejection seat trainer. The trainer was a cockpit, set up out on the ground, with a vertical track that protruded up about thirty or forty feet in the air. The student entered the cockpit; strapped himself in as though he was in an actual cockpit, pulled his visor on his helmet down, pulled the left arm rest up that locked his harness and ejected the canopy, pulled his right arm rest up that armed the trigger and the firing mechanism; and then with his head pressed firmly against the head rest, he squeezed the trigger. This fired the shell at the bottom of the ejection track and sent the student up into the air to the top of the track. In many cases, he would let out a loud yell. In my class of approximately one hundred men, twelve tailbones were broken, thereby requiring the student to sit on a 'donut' cushion for most of his instruction rides.

During this training I carpooled with a fellow from New York who was an atheist. It appeared to me that he was determined to destroy my belief in GOD, for quite often; he would pull out his little testament and give me a certain passage of scripture and request that I explain it to him. Just before graduation, he told me that the answers that I gave him were the best that he had ever received concerning the scriptures. I admit that he kept me on my toes, but I had expected to discuss flying procedures, etc, instead of religion!

While in this basic flight school, one morning we were shocked to learn that one of our classmates had died over the weekend. Seems that he died of Cancer, after getting a cold. The Cancer spread to his lungs and quickly killed him. That didn't say much about our physical examinations prior to entry into training! Or else one of his close friends just happened to be a Flight Surgeon who performed his pre-entry physical examination.

This basic flight training was what I had dreamed about and waited for my entire life. This is where it all was located. I enjoyed this phase of training more than the previous two, and I quickly decided that it would be a tough job for the system to wash me out before I received my wings as a pilot! I would fight, tooth and nail, to graduate, and there would definitely be no resignation or quitting by me! One day after I had soloed in the T-Bird, I experienced a complete electrical failure while out flying by myself. One thing that is stressed every day in training is the practice, and use of emergency procedures. No matter what type of aircraft one flies, he must first learn the emergency procedures and show competence in carrying them out. Electrical Failure meant that I had no radios with which to talk to the tower and request landing instructions. I followed the emergency procedures to the letter, and as I entered the traffic pattern for landing, I rocked my wings, signaling loss of radio contact. I continued until the tower gave me a green light to land. Then I pitched out, which means that I went into a sixty-degree bank for a turn of 180 degrees; lowered my landing gear and continued the landing and the landing roll out or deceleration. No sweat! The procedure worked as written.

During my 115 hours of flying the T-33, there were several times when I was required to use the emergency procedures listed in our aircraft manual. Always the same result was obtained. The procedures were correct and worked like a charm. I was never required to abandon the aircraft by ejecting and parachuting to earth.

One stage of this training involved a series of touch and go landings without stopping. This training was described as shooting landing stages. Our wives were allowed to watch our landings as they were positioned near the runway mobile controller, which was a small tower-like device near the runway. I remember trying to put on a show for my wife, who, I later learned was not present. I would touch down on my main landing gear; hold the nose wheel off the runway, while making another take off. This I did for about six landings in order to finish the stages. The mobile tower operator would tell the ladies who the next pilot was as we kept landing one after the other. I was really disappointed that my wife did not come to the base to witness my progress.

One of the subjects in this phase of training involved formation flying. This meant that our wings were tucked inside the leader's wings, and all signals between the aircraft were hand signals without radio chatter. We were so close to one another that we could see the other pilot when he blinked his eyelids. He wore an oxygen mask, but we could tell when he talked by the movement of his mask up or down. I did my early training in formation with an instructor who was not my personal one. He told my instructor that I would have no trouble soloing in formation, for I didn't get close enough to be dangerous. That really got under my skin! In fact, the day that I soloed in formation, I was in a flight led by our Flight Commander. As I tucked my wing inside his, he motioned, with his hand, for me to move out; I was too close for his comfort! I had to smile on that one.

Unknown to me, I was in the running for number one in the class. This was determined by all scores received, in class work and tests, flying grades and military scores. However, on my last formation flight, I encountered a tough situation. I was solo and number three in a four-ship formation. Being number three in the formation meant that number four was on my wing. My wingman was also solo and was spastic in his handling of his aircraft. He was up and down, close then far, and very unsteady with his control. I was almost sure that he would collide with me before the flight was finished. His unskilled handling of his aircraft caused us both to be late in joining up with the leader who, of course, had an instructor in that plane. Since I was leading number four into the formation, I was graded down for a slow join up. This cost me the Commander's Trophy.

While on my last cross-country flight with my Flight Commander, we flew from Laredo, Texas, to MacDill AFB, Florida. Thence, to Memphis Naval Air Station in Memphis, Tennessee, where we spent the night with my brother and his family. Then we returned to Laredo AFB, Texas. On this last leg, my Flight Commander wiggled the stick and said to me; "I've got it, its mine." I came off the controls and gave the bird to him. We were flying at about 30,000 feet altitude, when he rolled the plane over on its back, dropped the speed brakes, and went diving for the Earth. We were over a ranch in Southwestern Texas, and I saw what his object was. There was a cow standing on the dam of a small pond or lake. We were very near the ground, running at about 80% of the speed of sound which put us over 600 miles per hour. The cow neither saw us coming nor heard us! As we passed over the cow, he pulled the aircraft nose up and we were climbing like a bat out of a cave! With our tail pipe pointed at the cow, the sound must have been almost unbearable! A quick glance backward showed us that the cow had jumped off the dam and into the lake. She probably hasn't given any milk since!

There were one hundred men in my pilot training class, and all were commissioned officers that had held other flying jobs and positions. Since I was determined to complete this training for which I had waited all my life, I applied myself diligently to study, memory-work, and following my instructor's suggestions and methods. I was fortunate to graduate as the number two man in my class, and earned the designation,"Distinguished Graduate". This, later, won me a Regular Commission, which is the same as a graduate of one of the Military Academies. Work pays off!

Since I graduated second in my class, I got the second choice of all the assignments. Since I already had five to six years in the USAF, I wanted to build my flying time up quickly, so I took one of only two assignments to transport aircraft, a C-118. This is a four-engine propeller driven aircraft that flew internationally out of McGuire AFB, New Jersey. I had no desire to bomb, strafe or fly in close support of ground troops. I did not want to kill!

This decision got me a transfer to West Palm Beach, Florida, for two to three months of learning how to fly a four-engine airplane. What a change from that single engine jet airplane. This was quite an experience! While training there, I learned that my instructor in Basic Pilot School,

Allen McNair, had been discharged from the USAF and was operating a Western Auto Store in West Palm Beach. I took him out to a small airport and gave him lessons in flying a "Bug Smasher". A Bug Smasher is a small single engine civilian airplane of two or four seats with a high wing. The jet that he taught me to fly had a low wing. The Bug Smasher's top speed is about 150 miles per hour. We had a lot of laughs during our flight and had a lot of smashed bugs on our windshield!

CHAPTER V
FLYING THE LINE

Following the C-118 or DC-6B transition training at West Palm Beach, Florida, I was transferred to a Transport Squadron at McGuire AFB, New Jersey. This type of flying was called "flying the line", with flights to Europe, the Middle East and the North Country of Labrador and Greenland. What an experience this was for me! On one occasion, during winter, we landed with four inches of ice on our windshield. I was only a co-pilot at the time, but how very impressed I was with the pilot. There is a small curved window between the windshield and the side window, and with it open, the onrushing air does not come into the flight deck but rushes by the opening.

With the weather window open, the pilot, by leaning to his left, can see forward without looking through the windshield. There is a tendency for the pilot to land the plane in a slight crab or off-center position at touchdown. Regardless, the old boy did a great job of getting the bird down safely and surely. I was impressed a great deal with his skill. Need I say that I was a bit concerned about the ice? Our wings were fairly clean of ice because we had wing heaters that kept hot air circulating through the leading edges of the wings and tail.

On one trip up the Eastern Seaboard to Labrador, we heard a co-pilot call in to Mont Joli Radio to give his position report. He kept calling the station by pronouncing Mont Joli Radio just as it appeared in writing. Several calls were made without any response or answer. Finally, after some five minutes had passed, the radio station finally answered. With a great deal of patience and long-suffering in his voice, the operator called the aircraft and stated, "Air Force 529, be advised that this is Moan Joe Lee Radio, go ahead with your report." Quickly the Air Force plane came back and gave his position report in French. With great patience in his voice, the Radio Station replied, "Be advised, Air Force 529, we don't speak French down here." Immediately, the Air Force co-pilot replied, "Roger, Mont Jolly Radio, now here is my position report, Sport!"

Many Navigators, Bombardiers, Intercept Operators, Performance Engineers, and other rated non-pilot positions later entered pilot training. Some were nuts that didn't graduate with pilot wings and some were nuts that did graduate. One particular nut, with which I was acquainted, came into our squadron and started flying the line with us. Each new pilot must serve a period of time as Second Officer (co-pilot), then First Officer (pilot) and finally, if he progresses normally, he will move up to Aircraft Commander. He must prove his proficiency in the cockpit or flight deck of the aircraft and in the cockpit of the Flight Simulator. Emergency procedures must be impeccable and correct to a gnat's eyebrow!

This nut was flying transatlantic as co-pilot on one particular mission. He was allowed to operate the radios and learn how to make position reports while over water, enroute from Europe to the United States. The aircraft was controlled by the autopilot, and the crew tried very hard to make the flight as smooth and as boring as possible for the passengers' benefit. These flights were flown to shuttle military members and their families to and from Europe and the United States.

On this particular flight, the Aircraft Commander, who always used the left seat, got up, advised the nutty co-pilot that he was going to check on the passengers, and then go to the latrine, (rest room), in the tail of the aircraft. He made his way slowly down the aisle, chatting occasionally with those who were awake and talkative, and finally entered the rest room in the aircraft tail. This was near the galley where meals were prepared and was the area of the Flight Attendants. After closing the rest room door and preparing to ease his pain, suddenly, the aircraft went into violent maneuvers wherein the aircraft acted like a porpoise or dolphin. Nose up, nose down, some people left their seats involuntarily, suspended in mid-air, and many became alarmed and started yelling. Not to mention the actions of the Aircraft Commander in the rest room. In the tail of the aircraft, sudden movements are definitely accentuated and felt with increased movement!

As the aircraft pitched and rolled about, the Aircraft Commander came tearing out of the rest room, and went flying up the aisle at full speed. Quickly, he jumped into the left seat and stated, "O.K. I have the aircraft." Then he noticed that the autopilot was turned off. He looked at the co-pilot, who had a sheepish grin on his face, and who said, "Did you wet on yourself?" The Aircraft Commander was fit to be tied! He told the co-pilot to vacate his seat and get the pilot back in there for the rest of the mission. The co-pilot caused the violent maneuvers, intentionally; to shake up the AC, and make him wet his pants! How stupid!

On another trip to Europe, the First Officer or pilot was also a joker of the first magnitude. He decided to take a break from the cockpit, stretch his legs and visit the cabin. On these military aircraft, the passenger seats always faced the rear of the plane. The pilot donned his overcoat, gloves and a scarf before he entered the passenger compartment. He pulled a stocking cap over his head and made his way into the main cabin.

As he beat his arms with his hands, as if he were extremely cold, he encountered a lady passenger coming up the aisle.

She was looking intently between and under each row of seats. She said to him, "Sir, have you seen my little boy? He went down the aisle a few minutes ago, and now, I can't seem to find him. I'm very worried!" The pilot beat his arms again, and said to the lady, "Well, Ma am, I've been out on the wings, and he wasn't out there. He must be somewhere inside this vehicle. I'll help you look for him." Eventually, the young man was found and was required to put on his seat belt, and stay with his mom for the remainder of the trip.

On one occasion, during a flight from Europe to the United States, I was in the co-pilot's seat. It was nighttime and on the flight deck, all lights were red. The instrument panel, overhead panels, and all radio and in-flight equipment were on with red letters, positions and switches glowing in the dark. The red lights are used to keep the eyes of the flight crew acclimated to seeing in subdued light without being blinded. I heard a noise in the space between the pilots' seats where the Flight Engineer sits. I turned to look into the darkness of the crew rest area and saw something move, but all that I could make out were four eyes and two sets of teeth. Then a voice said, "Man, these pilots must really need to know what time it is. Just look at all them crazy clocks!" I finally figured out who was back there. It was two young black soldiers whom we were transporting back to the U.S.A. and who had never seen the cockpit or flight deck of an aircraft.

While stationed at McGuire AFB, it was found that I had a bi-lateral hernia that had plagued me since High School. I was examined by six navy doctors at Philadelphia Naval Base and operated on at Ft. Dix Army Post. McGuire AFB had no hospital. I was given a thirty-day convalescent leave, and one day I happened to go by my Squadron offices. As I walked past a window, I saw the Squadron Commander motion to me to come into his office. He advised me that he had several openings for an Electronics school at Keesler AFB, Mississippi, and thought that I might be interested. After thinking about it for a very short time, I advised him that I would volunteer for it. I didn't care much for my assignment as a transport driver in his squadron. I didn't enjoy living in New Jersey very much. Soon after this decision, I was transferred to the new school.

CHAPTER VI
LEARNING HOW TO CHANGE A FUSE

Since I was born and educated in Mississippi, this gave me an opportunity to visit with friends, family, and acquaintances prior to entering classes.

This school seemed, at first, to be more than I had bargained for, because the study of electronics never really appealed to me. This training involved classroom work, eight hours per day for one full year minus one week. I really had to hit the books hard and burn the midnight oil much too often to my liking. I did better in the school than I had expected and wound up being selected for additional training with Industry at College Park, Maryland.

During my schoolwork at Keesler AFB, Mississippi, I was required to keep my flying up-to-date, and found myself flying as co-pilot in a DC-4 aircraft that we referred to as a C-54. This was a four-engine propeller driven aircraft, the workhorse of the Berlin Airlift of days past. Some of these aircraft had actually been used in the "Airlift" because we saw coal dust in the interior and baggage compartments. Since they were so old, we handled them with care!

On Saturdays, I was able to check out in a "Bug Smasher", a Cessna 172 aircraft that had room for a pilot and three passengers. I then flew charter flights from Gulfport, and Biloxi, Mississippi, to New Orleans, Baton Rouge, and other nearby cities. It seemed that Southern Airways, that serviced Gulfport and Biloxi had booked more seats than their planes had. This worked great for the owner of the small planes, and me, since I was paid to fly them. I also checked out in another small bird in the Keesler AFB, Aero Club, which was a Piper Tri-pacer. I used it to fly my family around and to visit our relatives. My three-year son got his first flying lesson on one trip. He had to stand up in order to reach the small wheel that we called "the stick", but he had a great big grin on his face while we experienced some up and down maneuvers. My first daughter, only one year old was restricted to the rear seat with her mom. On one trip, I was fortunate to be able to give my aged mother her first and only airplane ride. That was a thrill for me!

One day, while I was logging my four hours of monthly flying time, that was required each month in the DC-4 aircraft, I noticed something within my left eye that resembled a piece of broken glass. Rubbing the eye and wiping with Kleenex didn't seem to help much. After two days of this, I finally went to see the Flight Surgeon at the base. He promptly sent me to see an Opthmologist who was one of his off-base consultants. This good doctor, after a quick examination of the eye, said to me, "This is not a laughing matter!" At which I responded, "I'm not laughing." He picked up the phone, called the Ophthalmologist on the base and said, "Admit him now or he will lose the eye!"

The diagnosis was, a central retinal vein occlusion of the left eye, and I was admitted immediately to the hospital at the Air Force Base. I was kept there for about one or two weeks, and the treatment was the use of anti-coagulates to break up a blood clot in the Central Vein in the eyeball.

Blood was coming into the eye, but couldn't get out due to the clot in the vein. All the other veins and capillaries were rupturing and the "broken glass" that I had seen was actually blood cells in front of the retina.

I am very happy to say that the medications broke up the blood clot and my vision returned to 20/20 in the eye. My right eye was unaffected throughout the ordeal.

Then, the good old USAF sent me to additional electronics training in College Park, Maryland. This was an advanced electronics school with Industry, which lasted about five months. My wife was expecting our third child, and had to leave me early in order to travel via train to her parents' home in San Benito, Texas. I finished the school, which prepared me for my next assignment as Detachment Commander of an electronics unit at Point Barrow, Alaska. Finally, joining my family in South Texas, our third child, daughter number two, whom we named Diana, was born. There were only a few days to be with my family, for the long trip to the Northern most point in Alaska was pushing me to leave. My in-laws helped my wife and children to get settled near them, and then my travels began once more.

CHAPTER VII
UNDER THE AURORA BOREALIS

My journey to Point Barrow, Alaska, was preceded by stops and briefings at an Air Force Base in California, and also at Fairbanks, Alaska. It is simply amazing how much one must learn prior to beginning a new job or assignment. This job included my first experience at commanding any size unit other than an aircraft crew. I became the Commanding Officer of a detachment of men at Point Barrow. This was the unit for which I had been trained in Mississippi and Maryland. Barrow is a large Eskimo Settlement on the beach of the Arctic Ocean. There was a five thousand foot runway made of perforated steel, and there was only one approach aid to the airport. An airline flew into Barrow twice each week carrying mail and a few passengers. My arrival occurred in July, when the Sun was above the horizon all day.

During my time at Barrow, in the "land of the Midnight Sun" the year was broken up by; three months of darkness for twenty-four hours, three months of twilight or a normal day-night period, then three months of daylight for twenty-four hours continuously, and finally, three months of twilight or normal day-night periods. Of course, the weather was quite a bit different from what one normally experiences in the lower forty-eight states. In the winter months, a phenomenon known as a "White out" can and often does occur. This happens when the sky, the air, and the ground are all white. One has difficulty with depth perception, and outside it is easy to become disoriented and lost.

It became my lot to personally experience three episodes of this phenomenon during my year there. Each time this occurred, since it was winter, it happened in darkness. One has only one chance; remain inside the vehicle with the engine running, until a tracked vehicle can reach you to pull you out of the snowdrift during morning hours. Three of my nights were spent in this way! No one would ever leave their vehicle and attempt to walk to any place, for we observed Polar Bear tracks around our huts where we lived when not at work. Polar Bears will stalk a human and hunt him down for food.

Another phenomenon that fascinated me was the Aurora Borealis. Several times during the dark periods, my men and I were at work, repairing broken wire antennas, and would stop for a few minutes to rest. Even though the temperature was minus forty degrees Fahrenheit, we would stop work and lie back in the snow and rest. Believe me, I learned that even at a temperature this low, one can perspire. While resting we watched the Aurora directly overhead. It constantly moved and changed colors that appeared to be pastel. What a sight! There is absolutely nothing like it!

At our Detachment, we had a large antenna farm that we could change our reception distance by varying the frequency of our transmission. In cold temperatures, hoar frost formed on the wires to about six inches in diameter and sometimes caused them to break; hence, the repairs mentioned above. We had one antenna that was called a

Helix for it was shaped in a manner similar to a helix. It had a back-screen behind it that looked like a Ferris wheel, and it was mounted on a circular steel track. This configuration made it usable in all directions and it was steerable. Once, as the Moon came up over the horizon, we turned the antenna and aimed at it. With only a very short lead, we triggered the transmitter. We received a return blip in a short time, and by converting time elapsed before receiving the reflected signal to distance, we easily noted that the Moon was, indeed, only about 240,000 miles from the Earth.

One other time, we were able to send a signal, bouncing between the Earth and the Ionosphere completely around the Earth. This we referred to as an ATW or 'Around the World' signal. We caught the signal on the rear part of our antenna, converted time to distance, and measured the circumference of Planet Earth.

During the warm part of the year, when the Sun was up all day long, it was a common occurrence to see submarines that surfaced and were observing our site. In summer the, ice began to break up, melt and allow shipping in that part of the Arctic Ocean. From time to time, we saw Ice Breakers and other ships, some near enough for us to get a good look at them.

The camp of Quonset Huts, where we lived, was operated by Puget Sound and Drake Construction Company and was manned by men from the lower forty-eight states. One of these men, a fireman, became a close friend of mine. He learned that I liked to play a guitar, as did he, so he brought two guitars over to my hut, and we whiled away many hours after work. Our music was never pursued by Nashville, and since one half of this particular hut was mine, we had little complaining from next door.

In the Settlement of Barrow, there was one Doctor and one Dentist in the hospital. It appeared that the Doctor was educated at Vanderbilt, in Nashville, Tennessee, and the Dentist was also from the South. They both became my friends and we spent many evenings, talking, visiting and talking some more. In the village, there were no law enforcement officers. Once each month, during summer, a State Trooper would fly up from Anchorage or Fairbanks, hear all complaints, make arrests and assign jail terms. He acted as Sheriff, Prosecutor, Judge and Jailer.

One night in particular, I visited with my friends, the Doctor and the Dentist in the hospital. My friend from the camp, that played guitar with me, asked me to give him a ride back to the camp since he was visiting friends there in town. The village of Barrow was five miles down the beach from our camp and the airport. Following my visit, I stopped my vehicle, a World War II Army Ambulance that had aircraft tires on it, in order to get over both snow and sand. At the house where I was to pick up my friend, I stopped and left the engine running as we always did in cold weather.

Eskimo houses have a snow-break in front of the front door. This snow-break is like a closet that opens to the outside, ninety degrees in direction from the door of the house. It is almost always unlighted and stops the wind and snow from blowing into the house. I was wearing a heavy parka with heavy pants and Muk Luk fabric boots. As I stepped into the snow-break, I saw something white moving about. As my eyes became accustomed to the darkness, I could see that it was a male Eskimo, in a 'T-shirt, trying to force his way into the house. People on the inside were holding against the door, for they didn't want this man to come in.

He turned toward me and said, "Who the hell are you?" He started pushing me back out of the snow-break, as I replied, "I'm Jim Shouse. Who are you?" My answer did not go over well with him, and he pushed me back some more as he said, "You better go!"

I said, "Look, Fellow, I only stopped to pick up my friend and then go." He left and went into the house next door, which was only about twelve feet away, and I grabbed my chance. I ran into the snow-break, hammered on the door, and yelled to my friend that if he wanted a ride, he must come out now. I turned around and there was the Eskimo man standing in the doorway with a sixteen inch skinning knife in his hand. He began to jab me in the stomach as I backed away. I had nothing with which to defend myself but my mittened hands. He said," I told you to go!" He kept up jabbing me, and I didn't know what to do. When my hope for a way out of this predicament seemed to be lost, two Eskimo men came by, saw what was happening, and grabbed the man with the knife and said to me, "GO!" I quickly got in my vehicle and left without my friend. I found out later the reason that the people inside the house didn't want the man with the knife to come in, was because one day when the man of the house was working at the airport, this man came in and raped the working man's wife. The man with the knife was known as "Wild Willie." He was intoxicated, and even though Barrow was 'dry' as far as alcohol is concerned, the Eskimos drink like fish.

Once Wild Willie went into a widow's house and robbed her. All he got was a couple of dollars and some change. This made him so angry that he burned her house down.

Incidentally, Eskimos only live in igloos while hunting. They normally live in small two or three room houses.

During this year in Alaska, I saw the temperature go down to minus sixty degrees. I got homesick for my family, and decided that I never again wanted to live in a cold climate. While I was away from home, my son started to school in Southern Texas, and my second daughter, Diana, had no idea who I was when I returned. She wouldn't let me touch her without yelling, but she loved her Grandpa. It seems that my Service Career was one long series of interruptions from being with my family and home. My home was always the most precious to me, all through my growing years, and through the births of my four children.

CHAPTER VIII
SCHOOLBOY ONCE MORE

Following my tour in Northern Alaska, I returned home to a house full of Chicken Pox, and a young daughter who had no idea who this strange man was. With a few days off, I was then reassigned to the University of Omaha; now known as the University of Nebraska at Omaha, for entrance into the Bootstrap Program for completion of my undergraduate degree. This was done to keep a promise made to my parents prior to entering the USAF.

After an evaluation by the University, it appeared that I only needed twenty-four semester hours more in order to receive a degree. This was accomplished in one semester and one summer six-week term. The school was loaded with Bootstrappers, so I was at home with many from all branches of Military Service. I graduated with a 3.5 average and received a Bachelor of Science Degree in Education in a total of seven months of schooling.

During this time, my eldest daughter started to school in Omaha, while my second daughter still had not decided if I really belonged in her family. My son was in the Second Grade and growing rapidly.

Upon graduation from the University, I was transferred to a small Detachment in Denver, Colorado. This, of course, required me to attend more specialized schooling at Denver Research Institute and at Edgerton, Germinghausen and Grier in Boston, Massachusetts. The men who were picked for my Detachment attended these two schools with me. The training that we received was the 'cat's pajamas' of Electronic Training. We were to operate highly technical equipment in a large aircraft, which was manned by another flight crew. This required us to accrue a considerable amount of temporary duty at other locations from our normal base of activity. As for my flying expertise, I was quickly introduced to a DC-3 aircraft, a tail dragger with a tail wheel, for which I had never flown. We called this bird a "Gooney Bird" for it was built in the 1930's, and was made famous by Arthur Godfrey of television fame. Especially, since he buzzed The Teterboro Tower and caused quite a stir with his "Gooney Bird".

My experience in the Gooney Bird taught me a lot about the art of flying, especially in mountainous terrain. Once while on a local flight from Lowry AFB, near Denver, I encountered a Mountain Wave. This was my first time to really experience the effects of a mountain wave. This wave occurs when the air flowing over the mountains tends to follow the terrain in its movement. Since Denver is on the down side of the Rocky Mountains and is relatively flat terrain, the air coming over the peaks begins to dive toward the ground, and makes a horizontal roll of air that is vicious to say the least!

Suddenly, I found my aircraft descending rapidly, even though I had the nose pointed upward and had maximum power on the two engines. I kept descending until I made a turn back and away from the area. Then I found myself ascending rapidly, even though the aircraft nose was pointing down and power on the engines was at idle. The only thing one can do when this type of event is encountered is turn away, clear the area as fast as possible, and get away from the mountains.

Later, I learned how to spot the Mountain Wave, even though the wave is invisible. As the air flows over the peaks, it causes a small thin cloud, known as a lenticular cloud, to form at the top of the wave. It is small and easily overlooked, but announces approaching disaster to the unobserving pilot.

On one trip to Andrews AFB, Maryland, from Denver, I learned another quick lesson from the Gooney Bird. My co-pilot was a Colonel who had many hours in the DC-3. I flew the airplane to Maryland and the Colonel flew it back to Denver. We had a load of equipment and materials for off-load at Andrews. These materials were to be used by the Air Force Academy Cadets at a briefing that they were to give.

Everything went o.k. except that the way the load was put on board made the old bird tail heavy. We managed to make it safely to Andrews and unload. The next day we set out for Denver again with the good Colonel doing the flying. Since as co-pilot, I was handling the radios, I learned that Lowry AFB, at Denver, had strong crosswinds on the runway. We were restricted from attempting a landing when the crosswinds were above fifteen knots. In our case, the winds were fifteen knots with gusts to twenty-five.

I turned to the Colonel and said, "Looks like we had better plan on landing at Peterson Air National Guard Base; which was also at Denver, but with longer runways and more aligned with the winds. The Colonel just looked at me as an inexperienced pilot who was being ultra conservative with the airplane. After all, I was the Aircraft Commander, and was responsible for the aircraft and the crew. He said, "Nah, we'll make it fine at Lowry AFB."

I thought, maybe he knows how to fly this bird better than I do, but I don't like this one bit! We entered the traffic pattern at Lowry, and soon were on final approach to the East Runway. He not only had to keep one wing low into the wind, but also had to "crab" the plane more into the wind. We were almost flying sideways. Since I was in the co-pilot's seat, and with the plane crabbed to the left, I was looking squarely down the centerline of the runway.

He started to flare for touchdown when we hit and bounced; then hit again and bounced again as we neared the left side of the runway. My hands kept reaching for the 'yoke', but I did not take over. Finally, the Colonel yelled to me, "Help me, Dammit!" With that, I was on the controls with him, and also on the rudder pedals and brakes. I pushed more power to the up-wind engine, pulled the right throttle to idle and stood up on the brakes. We finally stopped on the runway, but couldn't taxi to the ramp because of the strong winds. We called for transportation and a tug to remove the aircraft from the active runway. Yet, I doubt seriously if anyone ever tried to land at Lowry that night. Whew! I determined, then and there, to never allow a co-pilot to talk me into doing something against my better judgment! After a short tour at Lowry, my crew of trained electronics operators and I were transferred to McClellan AFB, California.

CHAPTER IX
ELECTRONIC MARVELS

Our move to California was both interesting and eventful. My team and I continued our operations and work, but from a different viewpoint. Again, we were involved in many temporary duty locations in the Pacific area. We became familiar with the islands of Hawaii and many other places in the Pacific Ocean. For instance, on one trip to Midway Island, we became familiar with living "Gooney Birds". These large birds of the Albatross Family were entertaining to watch. They winter each year on Midway Island and spend several months out at sea where fish are plentiful and easily caught. When they return to land at Midway, they often forget to put their feet down and land on their bellies.

When these birds fly over a person on the beach, they turn their heads, looking back at the individual and fly into a palm tree. When landing on their bellies, they slide for a distance, and I got a lot of laughs while watching them. I was told that at mating time, they will make their nests on top of the ground. There is no straw or brush in their nests, just sand wallowed out by their bellies. I saw one Gooney rise and leave its nest, and I could see that the only thing in the nest was a soft ball. Another was sitting on a nest with a coke bottle in it. Their crazy and highly unusual conduct is why they obtained the name of "Gooney Birds."

While at McClellan AFB, my fourth child and third daughter, who received the name, Joni, was born at home. My wife called me at work to come take her across town to the hospital at Mather AFB, since McClellan AFB had no hospital. I drove her to the hospital and waited while she was seen by the doctor. He told her that she was in labor, but had not dilated enough to deliver the child. He sent her home. I tried to get her to let me talk to the doctor, since she had already given birth to three children earlier. The second and third children were delivered rather quickly, and I expected this one to be no different. She was hurting and wanted to go home, so she didn't want me to talk with the doctor.

We returned across town to our residence, she went to bed, and I hurriedly went to McClellan to sign out on leave for the maternity. A very good neighbor, who was the wife of a Flight Surgeon, and who was a Registered Nurse, her name was Joni Schneider, just happened to come by to check on my wife. As she entered the bedroom where my wife was in bed, she found her giving birth to our daughter alone. She helped with the delivery, called an ambulance, and took care of our other three children. As I drove up, returning from the base, my son met me and said, "Dad, Mother has already had the baby in the bed room." I sent him to Mrs. Schneider's house and jumped into the ambulance.

It happened that it was rush hour for quitting time and traffic was atrocious! The ambulance driver drove over islands in the streets and through gas stations, to get around the traffic, for even with siren and red lights going and the ambulance horn blowing, people just would not clear the way for the ambulance! My wife had lost so much blood that the attendant kept telling the driver to hurry. I even put my head out of the window and yelled at the other drivers to yield the right of way. Nothing helped.

The doctor who had sent my wife home was a doctor named Christian. My wife required two or three blood transfusions after arrival at the hospital. Need I say that they almost lost her? I was near enough to hear, even though they had pulled curtains around her bed, so that I couldn't see what was happening. Since the child was born at home, she was not allowed in the nursery. The good doctor, by name, Dr. Christian, came out to me and explained that she almost didn't make it for loss of blood, but that they now had her stabilized. I requested his name. He said, "It is Christian." I replied, "Doctor, I will be in the office of your boss at 8:00 A.M. tomorrow morning." He said with a sneer, "Fine. Just be sure that you spell my name correctly."

Finally, my wife and daughter, Joni, were moved off the ward and put in a private room. I can honestly say that I have never seen a hospital room so filthy as was this one! They put our daughter in a crib that had many ants in it. The door facings were filthy with fingerprints and grease smears. I went to my Squadron and reported this to my boss. I was told to not go to the Hospital Commander and complain, for little good would come of it. Instead, I was to document all the items listed above, and send it to my Squadron Commander. He would add his endorsement and comments and forward it to the Hospital Commander. He did just that, and I still have a copy of the Hospital Commander's return letter to me wherein the following actions were taken. One, the hospital doctors were forbidden to send any woman home, thereafter, who had already started labor.

Two, the hospital rooms were fumigated to kill ants and insects, and finally, the interior of the rooms were cleaned and painted. Though this helped us none, it did help the next mother who checked in there. Incidentally, the Flight Surgeon's wife, Mrs. Joni Schneider provided our daughter with her first name.

Later, when Joni was about three months old, my wife and three of my children came down with Influenza. Our doctor told me to get Joni out of the house, for the Flu would kill her. I farmed her out to some friends of ours who used to live near us. They kept Joni for about two months until she almost felt like part of their family instead of ours.

When Joni was ten months old, I noticed that as she watched cartoons with her brother and sisters, if I turned the sound off, she did not appear to notice a difference. I took here over to a stereo and turned the volume up loud. Her hand went out to the speaker as she felt the sound. I knew then that she was deaf, since her mother had contracted Rubella or German Measles during her early pregnancy. Our military doctor said that she could hear, but was retarded. I didn't believe him, so we had her tested for hearing. She was profoundly deaf. Later at the age of two years old, she was tested in San Francisco, and was found to be just under the rating of Genius. How about them apples? She started to school at the age of two, and now has a Master's Degree from Gallaudet University in Washington, D.C.

During my assignment at McClellan AFB, California, I found myself again flying a C-118 or DC-6B aircraft. This is the four engine, propeller driven aircraft, configured for passenger transportation, which I had flown immediately following graduation from USAF Pilot School. This flying involved carrying teams of people throughout the United

States. On one particular trip to the East Coast and return, I made a stop in Dallas, Texas, to on-load some passengers who were returning to California. After take off, all engines appeared to be operating correctly until we passed over Albuquerque, New Mexico. At this time, I noticed that number one engine's cylinder head temperature was slowly creeping above the normal range. I told the Flight Engineer to cool the engine down. He quickly adjusted the engine cowl flaps to a more open position; thereby, lowering the head temperature. As the flight progressed, the Engineer found it necessary to keep opening the cowl flaps on that engine. After awhile, the cowl flaps, that allow more air to flow over the cylinder heads, were completely open. From then on, reducing power to the engine controlled the temperature. Incidentally, the number one engine and number two engine are on the left wing of the aircraft, while number three and four are on the right wing.

Before flying much farther, we found that the number one engine was not pulling its load, but was only idling. We kept it turning so that the passengers would not become scared or alarmed. But as we started to fly over Utah, the number two engine began to backfire loudly. This really got my attention! Just a little longer and we would have been over the mountainous terrain and could make it to our base at Sacramento, California. However, when number two started backfiring, I immediately made the decision to land at the nearest available airport. This had me making an approach, at night, in clouds, to Cedar City, Utah.

Cedar City is a small airport with no control tower and only one approach aid that is definitely not a precision device. The runway was stressed for forty-five thousand pounds and my aircraft weighed eighty-eight thousand pounds. With two engines inoperative on the same side of the aircraft, I had to fly with the wing slightly down, and crab the aircraft a few degrees in order to maintain a straight track over the ground and aligned with the runway.

Touchdown was uneventful and the runway was not damaged in any way. During our descent out of the clouds, the radio station at Cedar City, broadcast that a USAF aircraft was about to make a crash landing at the airport, so we had quite a few spectators watching as we made our approach and landing.

Several Highway Patrolmen were present and volunteered to take our passengers to a motel for the night. Others helped my crew get lodging, and I put in a phone call to my home base. Next morning, another aircraft arrived to pick up my passengers and take them on home. A mechanic was brought to us who helped get the two engines repaired and tested. We took off and returned safely to our home base in California.

Once, on takeoff from Warner-Robbins AFB, Ohio, near Dayton, we were climbing to our cruise altitude of eighteen thousand feet when I noticed a faint black smoke descending toward us. This was a jet-powered airliner descending from higher altitude for an approach and landing at Dayton, Ohio. The Air Traffic Controller, who was directing the airliner, mistakenly was descending him through our altitude. I declared an emergency on the radio, and turned our aircraft away from his track. Then after the collision was averted, I reported the incident to Air Traffic Control. Later, I learned through the grapevine that the Controller who was responsible for our "near miss" was relieved of his duties.

I might mention that the Aircraft Commander of a USAF aircraft always sits in the left seat while the co-pilot is in the right seat. The Aircraft Commander or AC as we called him, was known as the pilot. On transport planes, the AC usually takes his microphone and briefs the passengers as the plane is climbing to cruise altitude. He also points out items of interest as they fly over them. One AC was giving a very professional briefing to his passengers; for example, when he said, "If you look out the right side of the aircraft, you will see that we are passing over Yosemite National Park. And if you will look out the left side of the aircraft, you will SEE THAT NUMBER ONE ENGINE IS ON FIRE!

On another trip from California to Maryland, I began to have symptoms in the left eye similar to the one experienced in Mississippi. A quick trip to the Flight Surgeon was in order, and I was admitted to the hospital there and treated with anti-coagulates. It seems that I had experienced another flare up of the Central Retinal Vein Occlusion in the left eye. The next day, the occlusion or blocked vein was cleared up; I was released, and returned to my base in California.

Early one morning, I entered the large latrine, or men's bathroom, in the building where my men and I worked. I noticed that all the stalls were closed and occupied. As I was combing my hair, one of the men in a stall, called my name. He cracked open the stall door slightly, and said to me, "Captain, may I go home on an errand?"

I asked, "What kind of an errand?"

He replied, "I need to change my clothes!"

I asked, "Why do you need to change your clothes since the day is just beginning?"

He answered, "Well, since the latrine is so busy this morning, I decided to make a courtesy flush of my commode, and the danged thing overflowed on me, my clothes, and my shoes."

By this time, I was laughing so hard that I could hardly speak, and laughter was coming from each of the other stalls also. Finally, I gave him permission and quickly headed for my office, all the while laughing heartily.

On one particular flight to the East Coast, my Flight Engineer spoke confidentially to me about our co-pilot. He told me that I should watch the co-pilot perform the functions that I called out to him during the flight. And to watch him very carefully. It seems that he was a nervous type and sometimes grabbed the wrong levers. Sure enough, on the return leg of our flight, as we were landing at our home base, I saw him, out of the corner of my eye, reach for the wrong lever. After touchdown, and while lowering the nose wheel to the runway, I called for "reverse". This is a command to the Engineer to set the propellers for reverse pitch, so that the propeller blades stop biting into the air in front of us and began acting like an air brake to slow us down.

I then called for "flaps up" to the co-pilot. From the corner of my right eye, I saw him reach for the landing gear handle. Immediately, my right hand came off the throttles, and grabbed him by the wrist. Had he pulled that lever up, our landing gear would have collapsed, and we would have gone speeding down the runway on our belly, with sparks flying and parts of the aircraft coming off. I said nothing to him and finally released his arm. He looked at me and very sincerely said, "Jim, I'm so sorry. Thank you."

One day, the time for my annual check ride came up. This occurs when a Flight Examiner Pilot goes on a trip with the aircrew, supervises everything that the Aircraft

Commander does and says, and questions him at every turn on his knowledge of the aircraft and all of the emergency procedures. This was a two-day trip to Montgomery, Alabama, with a return the following day. Everything went well the first day, but on our return, as we passed over a radio station called, Jack's Creek Radio, we were hit by two lightening bolts squarely on the nose of the plane. This occurred over the State of Tennessee.

Believe me, one can see a bolt of lightening coming toward you. We were in thin clouds and these bolts came from very heavy static electricity. It appeared like a huge ball of fire that splattered over the nose and windshields of the plane. Then down the aisle, between the seats, a ball of fire rolled. The engineer had stepped off the flight deck to go to the rest room, when the ball of fire went rolling down the aisle. The ball passed between his legs as he tried to jump over it.

The ball of fire then exited the aircraft, and in its going, it knocked a large hole, approximately two feet in diameter in the rudder, knocked holes in both ailerons, which are the wing control surfaces, and scorched the hinges on both wings. I must say that this not only got our attention, but also pushed me into declaring an emergency and making an emergency landing at Scott AFB, Missouri, which is near St. Louis. Our home base diverted an aircraft to pick us up and return us home, and the aircraft remained at Scott AFB for a month while it was undergoing repairs. Lightening can, and does, strike twice in the same place!

On a mission, when my electronics crew of men were with me, over the Pacific, in a large aircraft that I was not piloting, the aircraft suffered a failed engine, forcing us to make an emergency landing on Christmas Island. There was no actively manned control tower there or Air Traffic Control of any kind. We had to fly low, over the runway, or buzz the field to scare a flock of sheep away before we could land. Parts were flown out to us from another base, the mechanic repaired the engine, and we finally returned to our home base. On another flight over the Pacific Ocean, we noticed that a fighter aircraft from another country was flying very near our left wing. He was close enough so that we could see the pilot blink his eyes. We merely waved to him, and since I had a camera, I took a picture of the pilot and his plane. The next day, the picture that I took was on the desk of Dean Rusk, our Secretary of State at that time.

Then one day, the previous trouble that had plagued my left eye, flared up for the third time. This time I was hospitalized at Travis AFB, in California, and began co-agulant therapy. Each morning, I was required to go to the laboratory and have blood drawn to check the Prothrombin time, (clotting time). After about one week, my kidneys began to hemorrhage. This worried me somewhat, for now I was urinating blood! A couple of very loud calls to the nurse brought her running to my bedside. After explaining to her that I was bleeding to death and peeing blood, she quietly reassured me, calmed me and merely stopped the anti-coagulates. The bleeding continued for about two to three days, and I was required to drink one and one-half gallons of water each day. After cleaning up the bleeding, I was sent home, but was grounded from all flying.

Later, about five months or so, I was sent to Brooks Army Hospital in San Antonia, Texas, for an evaluation. I was put through the same tests that our Astronauts were, except for the Psychological Battery, isolation and human temperament. These tests lasted all day long for one solid week. My left eye was dilated and photographed many times. The findings of these tests indicated that there was no permanent damage to my eye, and there was no evidence that I had ever had a Central Retinal Vein Occlusion. What wonderful news! I was returned to flying status and flight pay, without losing any money! Thank you LORD!

CHAPTER X
COMBAT

In 1969, it came my turn to travel to Southeast Asia for my contribution to the Viet Nam War. I was assigned to an Air Base in Western Thailand by the name of Nakon Phanom, which we affectionally referred to as N.K.P. My job there was in the Wing Command Post, where we launched all aircraft. But, I have the 'tail wagging the dog', so I shall begin again.

Upon leaving my base in Sacramento, California, I was sent to a location in the Philippines for training in Jungle Survival prior to arrival in Southeast Asia. This training, not too distant from Manila and the Air Base to which I reported for training, was referred to by all as the "Snake School". Believe me, its name was no exaggeration of the truth, for we found snakes of many different kinds throughout the three days that we spent in the jungle, in places where I never expected to find them. Fore instance, in the bark of some trees!

Before leaving the Philippines, I was required to qualify with the M-16 Automatic Rifle and a handgun, a 38 Caliber pistol. This was always a fun thing for me, because as a child, I hunted often with both rifle and shotgun. In fact, at age twelve, I used my father's double-barreled twelve-gauge shotgun to hunt squirrels and rabbits alone in the woods near our home. Strange! As I grew older, I did not like killing animals and stopped my hunting. The only thing that I try to kill now is snakes, the very symbol of evil.

After completing the school, where we learned to live off those things that the jungle provided, and receiving instruction in Judo, Karate, Jui Jitsu and dirty street fighting, we were then allowed to continue to our next base of assignment. In my case, that was NKP, Thailand. This base was located on the bank of the Mekong River that separated Thailand from Laos and farther west was Viet Nam. The Ho Chi Min Trail ran down through Laos and Viet Nam. On all flights to "Nam", one had to fly over the "Trail" and skirt the country of Cambodia.

As mentioned above, I was assigned duty as a Command Post Controller. I would work six days on day shift, six days on second shift, six days on Mid-shift and then four days off in which I had to do my flying. While at NKP, my primary aircraft for logging time was the dear old Gooney Bird. However, our Wing Commander had a T-28, single engine propeller driven trainer, in which he could travel around Thailand and also log his flying time. We were all required to fly four hours each month. A friend of mine and I had flown this aircraft during Primary Pilot Training: therefore, we were also allowed to fly the trainer. This aircraft was also used by the Royal Thai Air Force as a dive-bomber and for several other tasks. It was fun to fly, had plenty of power, and was highly maneuverable.

One day my friend and I were both flying in this bird. It had tandem cockpits, low wing, and a good clear canopy over us. Since we needed to log flying time and were practically unrestricted, we would fly over the Mekong River and look for small fishing boats. Once, we spotted one, we would climb up to a decent altitude and approach the small boat from the rear. Then we would begin a dive in order to pick up speed, pass over the boat very low, pull the nose up quickly and open the throttle. As we passed over the boat, our prop-wash would blow the small boat over, capsizing it. Sometimes we were able to see a man in the water near his boat, violently shaking his fist at us.

Another time, I was scheduled to fly a Colonel to Bangkok in the same small aircraft. We took off at about noon, for the short flight to Bangkok. I was climbing out to our cruise altitude when the Colonel, who was in the rear cockpit, called me on the interphone and said with a great deal of suffering and concern in his voice, "Jim, take me back to our base, for I have to s----" On our return, I was laughing so hard that I could hardly fly the plane safely. After landing, a staff car met us, and took the good Colonel to the hospital. I parked the bird and got out.

That's when it hit me! I started vomiting and running to the men's bathroom and then to the Flight Surgeon's office. It seems that twelve of us who ate our breakfast at the Officers' Club got a good case of food poisoning. Apparently, we all ate ham and cheese omelets wherein the ham was spoiled. Now the laugh was on me! How disastrous it would have been if this had hit me while I was flying the plane! With both of us vomiting and with diarrhea, it would be almost a miracle to land the plane safely.

As mentioned earlier, my primary aircraft for flying was the dear old Gooney. On day an Instructor, who was checking me out in the bird, and I had flown down to Bangkok. As we started taxi-ing out to the active runway, I was in control of the plane. With such a strong tailwind, I had to ride the brakes much too often to please me. As we neared the end of the taxiway, we had to turn ninety degrees to reach the runway. With the strong wind now blowing across our path, I was unable to stop the plane from turning. Even by standing up on one brake and pushing the up-wind throttle open, the plane just kept turning. The Gooney's Rudder is quite large and in a strong wind, it is very hard to handle.

At this point, the Instructor Pilot also got on the brakes and throttles, and we did a complete three hundred and sixty degree turn around before pulling out onto the runway and starting our takeoff roll. This is called a "ground loop" and is embarrassing to the pilot. Oh, well, live and learn. Fortunately, the tower operator remained quiet, but I'm sure that he got a good chuckle out of this maneuver!

One memory of my year in Thailand is not pleasant in any way. At the start of my shift in the command post early one morning, at first light, we started launching propeller driven fighter and dive-bombers in a S.A.R. Mission. S.A.R. Stands for Search And Rescue of a downed pilot or crewmember. This was a flight of six aircraft with call signs of "Sandy 1 through 6." These planes were heavily loaded with bombs attached to their wings, small missiles or rockets were also carried and heavy machine guns were loaded to the maximum. These planes were used to locate the downed crewmember, sanitize the area to keep the enemy from finding the crewmember, and protect two large helicopters, called "Jolly Green Giants", who were there to pick up the crewmember.

The Sandys were excellent at their jobs and always in a hurry to reach the area where the downed crewmember would be talking to them on the small radio that he carried in his flight suit. Once the area was "sanitized", the Jolly Greens would make the pick up and return to home base.

On this particular morning, early, Sandy Leader started his take-off roll down the runway. The tower talked directly to us as take-off roll continued. Suddenly, the Red Crash phone at my position began to ring loudly. I snatched it up hurriedly and heard the tower operator telling the pilot of Sandy Lead that he was on fire.

The pilot responded, "I'm aborting take-off."

Since he was heavily loaded, he couldn't stop the aircraft.

The tower operator asked him, "Do you want the barrier?"

The pilot answered, "Negative"!

As he neared the end of the runway and since the aircraft was not stopping, he retracted his landing gear. The plane settled down on the runway and was sliding on the bombs under the wings! As he skidded off the end of the runway and onto the overrun, finally coming to a stop, the tower said, "He's now standing up in the cockpit and is cutting himself loose from the harness." Just then, we heard a series of explosions, and the tower operator started crying as he said, "He just blew up!" Bomblets and other live ammunition were scattered all over the runway, and we had to close the field for the rest of that day while demolition crews cleared up the mess. The young pilot gave his life because he was trying to not tie up the runway for the other planes. What a sorry sight and sad predicament! The downed crewmember had to hide from the enemy and wait for his rescue the next day.

On another occasion, during a strike in Laos, we had a plane shot down. He was the leader of a two-ship formation and was the Vice Wing Commander at our base. He parachuted to the ground safely, but was completely surrounded by the enemy who he was dropping NAPALM, which is jellied gasoline, on. All he had to defend himself on the ground was a two-inch barrel thirty-eight caliber pistol. We also had ground teams of friendly soldiers in the area. They reported hearing many gunshots in the area where the Colonel had landed. His wingman kept making low passes over the area, even though he had no more bombs or ammunition of any kind left. This was an effort to keep the bad guys away. Finally, the Colonel talked to his wingman on his radio and said, "If you have any more bombs, put one right on top of me. I'm already shot and lost." His radio then went dead as the enemy troops smashed it with their rifle butts. He was never heard from again.

I remember this man well, for he picked me up and gave me rides in his staff car many times. You see, we had no transportation for workers on the base, so we did a lot of walking. At night, we had to be careful or we might step on a snake on the sidewalk. These snakes were plentiful and deadly! They were Kraits with neurotoxic poison; that were called "three steppers", for theoretically, one made only about three steps after being bitten. One last comment on the good Colonel. His wife was present in Bangkok, on a surprise visit to see her husband, at the time of his loss.

One of the nicer memories of Thailand involved a place in the Northern Corner of the country called Chiang Mai. It was a small town or village bordered on two sides by Burma, and was the summer home of the King of Thailand. This was a place where we could fly up there and spend the night away from the fighting and military environment. There were good restaurants and hotels and bathhouses where a tired man could relax, get in a good sauna and slowly begin to feel like a human again.

While the year progressed and tedium increased, I was allowed to take a one-week vacation and spend three or four days at home with my family. This was exceptionally nice, except for the normal conflict that I had with my wife. It was wonderful to get away from the war activity, and spend some time with my children. As the year dragged on, a big highlight was the visit of Bob Hope and his big troupe of entertainers. One standout person with Bob was Neil Armstrong just after having walked on the surface of the moon. WOW!

While I did not fly close-air-support or dive-bomber missions, I did manage to fly twenty-five combat missions in several different aircraft including old Gooney, a fighter bomber, a Candlestick aircraft that dropped flares, marking targets for the bombers at night. I made many trips to Viet Nam with both cargo and personnel. Once, a small jet fighter almost ran over us in a Gooney Bird near Da Nang, Viet Nam.

During my tour in the war zone, I was selected for Special Career monitoring. When asked what that meant, my Boss and friend told me that it meant that I would be put up for a star or Brigadier General. At that time, I was only a major.

Thailand was wonderful for jewelry. I managed to buy several items for my wife, my daughters and other friends. Since I flew the plane to various places with loads of passengers, I was able to receive good deals. The shop owners knew this and gave me some good prices. One day in the town of Nakon Phanom, as I walked down the sidewalk, a vendor who had his wares laid out on a towel stopped me and tried to sell me his products. I was not interested in shopping or buying anything, and kept refusing him. Finally, he pulled out a large green stone that I learned was a green Amethyst of about ten carats weight. It was not mounted and the vendor handed me a brick and told me to hit it. I refused. He then wrapped the stone in cotton and placed a coin, a Thai Baht, on the ground. He then placed the stone, with point down on the coin, and hit it very hard with the brick. The stone was unhurt but the coin had a large dent in it. He only wanted five dollars for the stone, and since I refused, I have kicked my own fanny many times for not buying it.

I learned a hard lesson while flying the twenty-five combat missions in Southeast Asia. Believe me, one can see bullets coming up at an aircraft in flight. One day while crossing the Ho Chi Min Trail, I saw flashes on the ground that indicated gun fire, and immediately there appeared a large swarm of bees coming up and flying past my window; bullets! At night, when over the Trail, we ran with all lights off, both inside and outside of the aircraft. No need to tempt disaster!

On one flight in the dear old Goon, my boss was in the left seat as we returned from a flight to Bangkok. It so happened as we approached the NKP area, that many fighters and other combat aircraft were being recovered from their missions. This meant that we were put into a holding pattern to let the combat birds land first. Much to our dismay, it was the Monsoon Season, and we were holding in a very heavy rainstorm. The Monsoon Season in Southeast Asia is a once in a lifetime experience. While flying and encountering the humongous rainstorms, it's more like swimming through the sky than flying through it! The Gooney Birds seats are slanted backward and there is an escape hatch over the pilots' heads. This hatch leaked like a sieve, and soon we were soaking wet. Since the seats were slanted toward the rear, our fannies were soaked. The plane was bumping and grinding and turbulence was somewhat disturbing to say the least. I couldn't help but laugh at my Boss, who was trying very hard to keep the bird in a straight and level configuration. Finally, with great pleading in his voice, he yelled at me, "Jim, get me out of this mess!" While stifling a guffaw and a snicker, I was able to get us a different place to do our holding pattern. We left the bird after landing as two almost drowned rats.

In bringing this chapter to a close, I must add a few things about Thailand in general. What a surprise it was to me to walk down the sidewalk, especially in Bangkok, and meet strangers, and see them smile at me and sometimes speak. The people have beautiful smiles and friendly attitudes. While there, I only learned three statements in the Thai Language: a greeting, "*Sahwadee Kop*" which means, "Hello"; *Kuhn Sah bidey loo*, which means "How are you?" and finally, "*Pome lah kuhn* which means "I love you". Thailand is a nice country, hospitable, friendly and kind.

CHAPTER XI
WORLDWIDE FLYING

Upon departing Southeast Asia, I had hoped to be reassigned to my old organization at McClellan AFB, California, but much to my dismay, the old organization' forgot' to request my reassignment. Naturally, I was reassigned to a new base, Norton AFB, at San Bernardino, California. This meant selling our house, taking three children out of public school and Joni out of deaf school. The morning after my arrival at home, I was awakened by the phone. One of my brothers was on the line, telling me to get back home to my mother's place in Mississippi. She needed to relocate, and we finally decided to put her with my brother who had called me. She would remain there about one year and then relocate again.

After my return to my home in California, we moved to Riverside, California, leased a house and moved in. My new assignment was with the Inspector General's Office as a transport pilot. My job was flying I.G. Teams worldwide. Again, I found myself in the cockpit of the old DC-6B or C-118. I had many hours on the books in this aircraft, and advanced to Aircraft Commander quickly. Soon thereafter, I was moved up to Instructor Pilot and finally to Flight

Examiner Pilot. This entailed administering check rides to other pilots who had less experience in the C-118 than I.

We were climbing out, immediately following take-off from Norton AFB, one day, when it became necessary to take evasive action. It seems that a small light airplane, flown by a highly inexperienced pilot, was in our traffic pattern and on a collision course with us. This is known as a "near-miss" and required me to bank our aircraft sharply to avoid hitting the small airplane. There was a General Officer on board, and apparently, the evasive action spilled his coffee. After reporting the incident to Air Traffic Control, we continued our departure and climb to cruising altitude. I got out of my seat and apologized to the General for spilling his coffee. He asked if I got the license number of the small aircraft that we referred to as a bug smasher. I explained that the quick maneuver prohibited us from getting the number.

While at Norton AFB, I received an evaluation from Southern Illinois University, and discovered that I was eligible to enter their MBA Program. After enrollment, an Instructor from the University would come to our base and conduct classes on Friday, Saturday, and Sunday. Then, on Sunday, we would receive the mid-term exam on one subject only. Six weeks later, he returned for three more days of school during the weekend, and then we took the final exam. Between the six-week periods, we were to study our textbooks and prepare for the upcoming exams.

On a trip with an I.G. Team to Europe, we experienced loss of an engine on three separate occasions. This definitely got my attention! The first loss occurred over Germany and required an emergency landing, and some maintenance to repair the engine. As we started our return trip to California, we landed at Upper Heyford Air Base in England. The next day, we took off and headed back across the Atlantic Ocean. We had only flown about forty-five minutes when a second engine failure occurred. We returned to Upper Heyford and spent the night while the aircraft was being repaired.

The next day, we tried again and this time we made it out over the Atlantic. We were flying at night in light weather when I left my seat on the Flight Deck and went to the rest area, which is immediately behind the Flight Deck. I sat down at a table to eat my dinner when an engine began backfiring loudly! Please believe me! When out over the Atlantic, at night in light weather conditions, and with an engine back-firing loudly, it's enough to be the cause of some concern!

I dashed back onto the Flight Deck, advised the Navigator to give me an accurate position and contacted the Air Traffic Control Agency that was monitoring our flight, telling them that I was declaring an emergency. The Navigator advised that we had just passed the ETP Point. This is the point on our flight path that is equi-distant to our destination at Goose Bay, Labrador and to our departure point. This meant that we didn't have enough fuel for three engines on advanced power to return to Ireland. We checked the weather at Keflavik Air Base, Iceland, which was nearest to us, and found it to be two hundred feet overcast with one-half mile visibility. We headed for Iceland! The Flight Engineer kept the bad engine's propeller turning to keep from exciting and worrying the passengers.

It seemed like forever to reach Iceland, and we found the conditions above, but also with heavy rain and gusty winds across the runway. I briefed my crew that we would make an ILS, Instrument Landing System Approach, and if we did not see the runway, we would pull up and make another approach. If we missed seeing the runway on the second approach, we would pull up and get as close to the Irish Coast as we could before we ran out of fuel and had to ditch the aircraft in the ocean.

We began our approach with me flying strictly by my instruments while the co-pilot looked outside. I guided the bird down to two hundred feet above the ground, and the co-pilot said,

"I see nothing!"

I said to him, "I'm going down fifty more feet!"

He yelled at me, "No, No!"

I was already at one hundred fifty feet when he yelled, "I have the strobe lights and the runway!" I looked up from my instruments and started reducing power to the three good engines. Immediately, we were blown off course with the runway, which necessitated a bank while at low altitude. This is very dangerous! It is so easy to hang the low wing on something and cause a crash. I managed to get back over the runway and make a touchdown on a runway that had at least two to three inches of water on it.

We taxied to the ramp and shut down the engines, thankfully. I was supposed to sign the aircraft form to certify the emergency, but my hands were shaking so badly that I could not sign anything. I walked back into the passenger compartment, and the passengers all stood and applauded my handling of the emergency. I think that they were as glad as was I to be safely on the ground. The next day, following maintenance to the bad engine, we continued on to our eventual destination of Norton AFB, California.

My Boss and I decided to apply for an Airline Transport Pilot's License in the DC-6B, just in case we might need it after we had separated from the Air Force.

On one particular flight, we wound up at a base in Kansas where we picked up an FAA Flight Examiner. He first checked my boss, and didn't give him very many emergencies, just standard items. Then we landed and it was my turn in the left seat. Before take-off, The Examiner required me to make a walk around preflight check of the aircraft. This was to check my knowledge of the aircraft and all its systems. For instance, Engines, Pneumatics, Hydraulics, Electrical, Pressure and all other systems in the aircraft.

The Examiner said to me, "You seem to be nervous about this check ride. Why?" I explained that I didn't have a great deal of flying time in the DC-6B.

He asked me, "How many flying hours do you have in this aircraft?"

I replied, "Between two and three thousand hours."

He said, "The average flying hours of the pilots that I check are about twenty to thirty total hours. They can't afford to rent a plane this big with a crew for many hours." That stunned me and I had no more nervousness about the check ride.

We took off, with me at the controls. Before I knew it, we had electrical problems and an over-speeding propeller. Finally, we experienced hydraulic problems for operating the wing flaps and landing gear, and immediately lost the engine that was over speeding. We barely had time to clean up the aircraft, declare a simulated emergency, and approach the field when we lost another engine beside the one that was already shut down. Now, I was required to make a two-engine approach, without wing flaps or reverse thrust after touchdown. The landing was uneventful and he told us to park and shut down all engines.

To our relief, we both passed the check rides, and later our licenses were mailed to us, good for life. I failed to mention that prior to the check-ride, we both had satisfactorily completed a written test that took four to six hours. Whew!

I was in command of a flight that visited many islands in the Pacific Ocean, and believe me, it is a BIG OCEAN! We also landed at three different places in Australia; Perth, Alice Springs, and finally Brisbane. Then, also, we stopped in Taiwan or what was once called Formosa, two different places in Japan, and finally started our return flight to our home base. We were briefed on weather enroute, filed our flight plan and took off. Unknown to us or the Weatherman who briefed us, a Typhoon was forming between us and our planned stop at the Island of Guam. Naturally, we had to fly through the center of it. Oh, JOY!

There was so much turbulence on this flight that most of the passengers suffered from airsickness. Even some crewmembers, especially the Flight Steward and Stewardess, were very sick. Before long, nobody had anything left to vomit: yet, they still experienced the same nausea and discomfort. What a miserable condition in which to find oneself! Now we were constantly in clouds, precipitation, and unstable air, looking for a small dot in a huge ocean. Guam looks mighty small when flying in the conditions that we experienced. The Navigator was unable to use Celestial Procedures for the Sun and Moon were neither visible. His primary navigational aids were Pressure Pattern and Dead Reckoning. Somehow, he was able to steer us to that tiny dot on the surface of that BIG Ocean, and when we sighted

Guam, it looked beautiful and many thanks went skyward from many very tired and worn out souls.

Part of my duties as a Flight Examiner was training new pilots how to fly the DC-6B safely. This is a big shock to pilots who have never handled four throttles of a plane weighing 88,200 pounds upon landing. Some wanted to land nose first, too fast or too slow, or they would forget to configure the aircraft prior to touchdown. Usually, after a flight, I would be somewhat hoarse from shouting above the noise that was present on the flight deck. Sometimes the new pilot would forget to "round out", which is getting the nose up prior to touchdown, and we would bounce hard and very high. That's when I would yell, "I've got it, let go!" I would then take over, add power and fly the plane up to let the student try again. On this plane, the crew sits about ten to twelve feet above the runway or ramp when on the ground, so new pilots must get used to landing this high above the runway.

It came my unpleasant task to give a contemporary pilot in my section at the I.G. a check ride. He was very overweight and subordinate to me, and he was a favorite of my boss who cared little for me. Talk about a loaded deck! I didn't want to check him for he knew so little about the aircraft, and couldn't care less about learning things that he should have known. However, the lot fell to me, and I determined to give it my best shot. I didn't want to fail him, for I knew that my boss expected me to do just that, and would accuse me of harboring enough dislike for the fellow that I would be unfair, sort of like a personality conflict.

I was shocked at his lack of knowledge, not only of the aircraft and its systems, but also of flying rules and regulations in general. Nevertheless, I gave him a passing grade on the flight, and I do emphasize the word 'gave'. My boss was surprised at my actions and said so to me. The officer, in question, acted like he was the 'Cat's Pajamas' and strutted around the office. I have heard him 'bad-mouth' me to our boss, but I said nothing. This whole episode was distasteful to me, and I did not dwell long on the subject.

Next came a check ride for me that was administered during a two-day trip from Southern California, to Montgomery, Alabama, and return. I mention this again because I left out some items that were important to report. As we were passing over Jack's Creek Radio Station in Tennessee, while flying in strata-form clouds, we saw a large bell of fire coming right at the nose of the aircraft. It hit us, splattered about, and went rolling down the aisle in the passenger compartment. Then BANG! Another bolt came the same way and acted the same way. We had just taken two lightening bolts on the aircraft. The Flight Examiner went into the tail rest room, placed his eye up against a small window, and detected a large hole in our rudder. These bolts were caused by static electricity in the stratus clouds wherein we were flying.

Naturally, this called for emergency procedures, and we diverted our flight path to Scott AFB, near St. Louis, Missouri. An uneventful landing was made and after parking, we discovered the large hole about two feet in diameter in the rudder, and also holes in each aileron. Ailerons, to ground pounders, are the control surfaces on the wings and are used to bank the aircraft. All control surface hinges were burnt black. This required the aircraft to remain at Scott AFB for approximately one month while undergoing repairs. Another aircraft was sent to pick us up and return us to Norton AFB. As a note of interest, I passed the check ride.

After arrival at Norton, I got in my auto and drove to my home in Riverside. Then, I received the third bolt of lightening! My wife advised me that she wanted a divorce! This bolt hurt most of all! It seems that a good friend of ours was in San Bernardino painting houses during his vacation. He and his family were the folks who took care of my daughter, Joni, when there were four cases of Flu in our family. He had spent most of the weekend at my home while I was off flying. I had talked to him on an earlier occasion, advised him that my wife and I were going through a difficult time, and I requested that he not visit my family whenever I was absent. He said that he understood. Yet, here he was visiting and advising my wife while I was absent. I got a bit angry over this development and the next day or two, I had a heart-to-heart talk with him and terminated our friendship.

To make a long story short, I found myself living in the BOQ, which is Air Force Jargonese for Bachelor Officer Quarters. My home was my delight, and this hurt terribly. After almost a year of listening to attorneys haggling with one another, primarily about my salary and custody of our children, a divorce was granted! I promptly became a mole in my BOQ suite.

Later, I began to get out a bit and visit other people like my friend, who lived in Beverly Hills. He was a Reserve Air Force Pilot who flew often with me. I was told, by my boss, to write an article on this person and nominate him for "Reservist of the Year for the whole U.S. Air Force. I did just that, and was pleased when he was selected soon thereafter.

And coming with this honor was promotion to Brigadier General.

On one trip to Los Angeles to have dinner with a friend at Christmas, I started back home rather late. As I was driving on the San Bernardino Freeway, during the first rain of the rainy season, I saw something up ahead under an overpass. I was in the second lane from the left of a five lane road headed East, and when I recognized what the object was ahead of me, it was a car in my lane, stopped dead without any lights showing. I quickly hit my brakes and tried to steer to the right to clear the car, but my vehicle hydroplaned, thereby committing me to plowing into the rear of the stopped car.

The impact knocked the stopped car about thirty or forty yards, and he steered to the edge of the freeway. I had to exit my vehicle through the right door, and had just reached the edge of the road when another car plowed into mine. The driver was an old man whom I helped get out of his car and over to the side of the road. Then a small car, a Volkswagen plowed into the side of my car that had become broadside to the traffic lanes. This caused a total loss to my nine-passenger station wagon that was in excellent condition.

As soon as the police arrived, they sent us all to the hospital for check ups. The man who had caused the accident had been drinking and was unhurt even though he was in the car when I hit his car.

He said, "My car stopped running, and I was hitting my brakes to show brake lights.

In essence, his battery went dead, and he failed to steer to the side of the freeway. There are no brake lights when the battery is dead!

I suffered a broken neck, had large blood clots in my throat and neck, had a broken right thumb and cracked ribs. The old gentleman who hit my car had a fractured kneecap, and the occupants of the Volkswagen had bloody noses and bumps on their heads. I recovered.

Now that the divorce was final, my son and I moved up into the mountains above San Bernardino to a small town known as Running Springs. We rented a chalet, built on the side of hills, that had a wonderful view of the Air Force Base and the city of San Bernardino far, far below. Eric was enrolled in school there, and we learned to survive during the snowy Winter. The Chalet was built on the side of the hills so that I had to park my auto above the roof of the house. Then, it was down two flights of stairs to reach the front door. One day, following a heavy snowstorm, I had to go to my car for something or other. Before starting back down the stairs, I yelled for Eric to come outside, so that I could throw a large snowball at him. He stuck his head out of the door, and I threw quickly. The only thing that I hit was my tailbone as my feet flew out from under me, and I went bumping down both flights of stairs, incurring a broken tailbone as I went. One good thing, my son saw it and did not laugh, as far as I could see. The bad thing about it was I had to fly to Ohio that night and sit on a broken part of my spine.

While stationed at Norton, I received a promotion to Lieutenant Colonel, which was the rank of my Immediate Superior and Supervisor. There was a promotion party for all the new L.C.s at the Officers' Club, and as the party ended, several of us continued to celebrate a bit. It was at this point that my boss, who had a "little man" complex, had a run in with me over some silly reason concerning my date. He decided not only to confront me, but appeared to be ready for a more serious altercation. Fortunately, for both of us, his wife got him out of the club quickly. Unknown to me at the time, this started my downfall from the position that I held. It was only later that I realized how much he hated me, and was ready to destroy my career for which I had worked long and hard.

Then one day, I was sent on a mission to New Orleans Naval Air Station with a No-Notice I.G. Team. We spent the night at Barksdale AFB, Louisiana, then took off next morning and dropped in on the Naval Air Station. The team was going to inspect an Air National Guard unit on the N.A.S. After team drop off; we refueled and prepared to depart for our home base. My co-pilot, who was a wise guy and also a Lieutenant Colonel in rank, refused to fly if he couldn't send our stewards off base to get food to prepare on our return flight. He tried to hide behind flying safety. In essence, he committed Mutiny, refused two direct orders from me, his Aircraft Commander and refused to fly if he didn't get his way. I first tried to reach his supervisor on the phone and then my supervisor, but was unable to reach either of them.

So, I allowed him to dispatch the stewards and even though the return leg would normally be his, I ordered him to the co-pilot's seat. Enroute, I made a phone patch to my supervisor's office, and requested that he meet the plane when it landed. He did, and I explained what this officer had done, and requested that he be not allowed to command an aircraft that carried our teams or act as Aircraft Commander on any aircraft. In essence, this would 'ground' him.

An investigation was begun into the incident, and it looked as if this officer would be court-martialed. He was only six months from retirement. I just could not see him lose his retirement, so I went to the General, our Commander, and asked that the charges be dropped. This way, the wise guy could still retire and receive his retirement pay. That act cost me my job, for my boss was furious with me for showing anger to the pilot, and asked that I be removed from his department.

Before I was moved out of the department, my Supervisor's Boss came to me and ordered me to write my Supervisor's Effectiveness Report. It is these reports that get a man promoted or passed over for promotion. This is illegal under any military procedure or practice, and is ridiculous, to say the least. Of Course, I wrote the E.R. and prepared it for my Supervisor's Boss' signature. He was the one to sign it. I was often given orders to write something for them to sign, for having been a Commander, myself, I knew how to write Military Correspondence effectively as mentioned earlier in this book. Wouldn't you know it?? My boss got promoted to full Colonel, and of course he didn't know that I, his subordinate, had effectively gotten it for him. This is the most ridiculous thing that ever happened to me during my military career. Talk about having the tables turned on you!

I was moved into another office until a new assignment came in for me, and given a Commendation Medal by my new boss. It was obvious to me that this next assignment would be my last, and there was no way to save my career in the USAF.

CHAPTER XII
WRAP UP OF A CAREER

My final assignment was to a C-118 unit located at Wiesbaden Air Base, Germany. I was put to work immediately during my first week there by performing a job that nobody else wanted. My family and I were living in a boarding house while awaiting delivery of our furniture and household goods, and really had only some clothes with us at the time. My duties, during this first week, were to act as Commandant of Troops, during a movement of the 'colors', our flag, from Wiesbaden Headquarters to Ramstein Air Base near the city of Kaiserslautern in Southern Germany. The new location was in Bavaria near the French border. This was strictly a military procedure with pomp and splendor.

As Commandant of Troops, it fell my duty to conduct this service while standing at attention in front of the old Headquarters Building and taking down our colors for the last time. I marched two Squadrons of enlisted men onto the parade ground along with a brass band, and positioned them directly in front of the reviewing stand and the Cadre of Officers headed by a General Officer, who was Commander of USAFE or United States Air Forces in Europe.

After positioning the group, I ordered, "Retreat" to be sounded by the Bugler. This brought our flag down for the last time at this location. After this, our National Anthem was played by the band while we were at "Present Arms", which is rendering the hand salute. Next, came the German National Anthem, "Deutschland Uber Alles" which, much to my surprise, was the same melody as I had sung in Church many times, but of course, with different words. After this service, I marched the troops off the field, and gave them a good tail chewing for talking while in ranks. I'm sure that they left wondering just who this "gung ho" Colonel was!

My job at the new location, involved flying the C-118 aircraft all over Europe and the Middle East. After our furniture and household goods arrived, my son enrolled in school on the base, and we moved into an apartment. We tried very hard to get used to our new location. In only about five months, we found ourselves moving to Ramstein Air Base, the place of the new Headquarters for USAFE. We settled into a house in the village of Machenbach and tried to blend in with the local citizens. Now, I was moved up to head of the Pilot's Department in this SAM Squadron. SAM stands for Special Air Missions, for that was our type of operation. Our primary duty was the transporting of people all over Europe, the Middle East and Asia Minor.

Most of the time, we transported VIPs, or Very Important Persons, wherever their duties required them to be. Each year, Senators and Congressmen and Women from the United States would come over to Europe and require our services as they made trips, primarily shopping trips, to Europe to purchase Christmas Gifts. Our flights were made free of charge to these passengers. On one trip, I returned a load of these VIPs to Paris, France, where they were scheduled to board a jet tanker for return to Andrews AFB, Maryland, which is near Washington, D.C. I had a load of their baggage and gifts that they had purchased, so I just had their stuff unloaded and left on the ramp for their people to pick up and direct to the right place.

We flew missions in and out of the city of Berlin while it was located in East Germany. There were three corridors ten statute miles wide, leading from West Germany into Berlin. We were required to remain in the corridors even though large thunderstorms were positioned right in the middle of the corridor. That didn't leave us much room to maneuver around the weather. Also, the minute that we penetrated East German Airspace, there were two fighter aircraft of the East German Air Force positioned at our six o'clock position, i.e. on our tail, though much higher. If we wandered outside the corridor, we could have been shot down.

Usually, the flights commenced at Bonn, West Germany, and terminated at Templehof Airdrome in Berlin. Remember, this was at the height of the Cold War between the USA and the USSR. We did not see the fighter aircraft, but GCI, Ground Control Intercept Operators, who monitored our flight path, advised us of the company that we had on our tail.

Jet Aircraft belonging to the U.S. Air Force and countries that were our allies were forbidden to fly into Berlin. Only propeller driven aircraft were allowed in East Germany. One time, the USA decided to call the East German's and Russian's bluff, and dispatched a small two-engine jet transport, known as a Sabre Liner or T-39, into Berlin. Yes, they were shadowed by East German Fighters, but landed safely at Templehof Airdrome.

At Templehof, Hitler had the terminal built so as to provide an over-hang or roof for aircraft to taxi under and de-plane their passengers out of the weather. The pilot on this flight of the T-39 happened to be a friend of mine, who was a naturalized U.S. Citizen from the Netherlands. He was Dutch and a very good pilot. He parked and got out of the plane. On his way to the Operations office, to close out his flight plan, he was met by a Russian Major, who called him by name.

He said, "Major Hogandorf, if you take off and fly back to Frankfort, Germany, you will promptly be shot down!

This somewhat unnerved my friend, so he went into the Operations Office and called USAFE Headquarters at Ramstein AB. He told them that he and his co-pilot were going to return to Frankfort on a train. USAFE Headquarters told him to stand by, and they would call him back after they had checked with Washington. Later, they returned his call and ordered him to take off and call the Russian's bluff. Of course, he didn't want to, but he advised them that since there were three corridors out of Berlin, he planned to use the shortest one.

They said, "Negative! You will utilize the longest corridor."

By now, my friend felt like a clay pigeon in a shooting gallery.

The next day, he and his co-pilot took off and headed for Dear Old Frankfurt, down the longest corridor. They flew the jet near the stalling speed so as to appear on radar as a much slower, propeller driven aircraft. Everything was quiet until they reached the halfway point of the corridor. The pilots looked at one another, looked all around outside, and the pilot said, "Lets make a run for it!"

They had no more than got the throttles moved up, when there was an East German Fighter aircraft sitting on their left wing. He was tucked in so tight with their bird that they could see him blink his eyes and his oxygen mask wiggle as he talked to someone. My friend told me that all he could do was just wave at the pilot. The fighter moved all around, above and below the T-39 as if he was looking it over. They could not see his wingman, but knew that he was high and on their tail.

Suddenly, they looked toward Frankfurt and spotted the contrails of a flight of West German F-105 Star Fighters, orbiting over Frankfort and awaiting any action by the East German Fighters. Had they observed any hindrance with our T-39, they were set to attack the enemy fighters. As they got closer to the end of the corridor, the East Germans broke off and returned to their home base. Our T-39 had called their bluff and gotten away with it! My friend said that the sight of the F-105s contrails were beautiful to see and gave them hope of getting out of this predicament!

The next day, my friend visited a GCI site that had monitored his flight out of Berlin. The operator played a tape that he had recorded the previous day as they followed his flight and the two East German Fighters. The two pilots of the East German Air Force were talking to each other, and one said, "This doesn't look like a fighter aircraft, but more like a small transport."

His wingman replied, "It doesn't matter. Our orders are to shoot it down."

The other pilot replied, "But I can't see any guns or weapons of any kind anywhere."

"Just shoot it down," the other pilot said. By this time, they saw the contrails of the F-105s watching their actions, and they wanted no part of them! My friend then made the decision to start his retirement paperwork. He kept saying, "I'm too old for this. I think its time that I threw in the towel.

It was a shock to me to learn that our government put so little value on the lives of our crewmen."

About this time, my son, Eric, graduated from High School in Germany, and wanted to return to the U.S. for awhile prior to entering college. Since school was out, we brought my three daughters to visit us, while I took a forty-five day vacation. My wife planned our trips, as we wanted the girls to see as much of Europe as possible during their visit. As it turned out, we took them into six different countries, and they got a glimpse of England as they stopped there on the way to Germany. They were able to pick up souvenirs in each country that we visited. As they prepared to return to their home in Las Vegas, Nevada, I was able to talk their mother into allowing my oldest daughter, Anne, to remain with us for one school semester. She was always the one who had to look after her two sisters, and she needed a break for herself.

While serving my last assignment, as expected, I was passed over for promotion to full Colonel, and realized that my days were numbered in the USAF. This, of course, was no surprise to me, since I knew how my old boss at Norton AFB, had put an end to my military career. He did it by inserting in an Effectiveness Report on me that he either wrote or had someone write for him that: "In his continuous and zealous effort to produce superior results, Lt. Col. Shouse has, on occasion, allowed his temper to overrule his demonstrated superior ability to make sound decisions, and to direct the efforts of his subordinates. Consequently, these temper flares have impaired his effectiveness in his current position." These two sentenances were the " kiss of death" to a career that had been rewarding and diligently pursued. It only takes one Effectiveness Report of this kind to end any career, even though the man who wrote this report, or had it done, had more of a temper problem than did I. There, most definitely, was a personality conflict between my old boss and me. And, my write up of his performance, which I was ordered to inflate, resulted in his promotion to Colonel. That is most unfair, and I might add, illegal under military regulations.

It was my duty, to fly the Commandant of the USAFE Headquarters into Berlin one day. General David Jones was my passenger, who later became Chairman of the Joint Chiefs of Staff in Washington, D.C. After landing, the General came up to me, thanked me for a pleasant flight, and wished us a safe return to our home base at Ramstein. I informed him that we would be staying the night since the airplane broke upon landing.

He said, "But I didn't know that!"

I replied, "It was not enough to bother you with."

He was an easy Commander with whom to fly and work.

It came my duty to fly to Cologne-Bonn and pick up General Daughtery and his team, that were being transferred to Offutt AFB, Nebraska, and fly them to Frankfurt, Germany, where they would board a KC-135 Jet-Powered Tanker, on to Offutt AFB. General Daughtery was to become the new Commander of the Strategic Air Command (SAC). His staff numbered about thirty-five personnel and since the good Colonel was such a congenial and low-key Officer, we tried very hard to give them a nice flight.

Upon our arrival in the Rhein Main Air Base area at Frankfurt, we realized that a rain shower had ended there just prior to our arrival. So this meant that we would have a damp runway for touchdown. We made our approach and rapidly came to the point of touchdown. I began to "milk" the airspeed and attitude of the aircraft, and got the best touchdown of my whole Air Force flying career. The point of touchdown was so soft that the passengers did not know that they were on the ground until they heard the propellers go into reverse thrust, and the bird began to slow down. As soon as I had taxied to the ramp, and the stairs were put up to the door, I put on my blouse or tunic, hat, and started to the rear so as to stand at attention on the ground as the passengers deplaned. On my way down the aisle, I was met by General Daughtery who was applauding loudly.

He shook my hand and said, "Colonel, in my thirty-two years of flying in the USAF, I must say that your landing was the best that I have ever seen or felt. I thought that you had forgotten to put down the landing gear, it was so soft. Thank you very much!" This General is one of the nicest officers that I encountered during my career.

One of my duties was to fly the President of West Germany, His Excellency, Gustav Heinemann, and the Chancellor, Willie Brandt, from the capitol of West Germany, Cologne-Bonn, into Berlin. This occurred periodically, but they didn't fly together, always separately. President Heinemann was my passenger, along with his staff, on many occasions. Even his daughter, Frau Uta Reine-Heinemann was also our passenger several times. While I was stationed in Germany, The President retired from office, and had his farewell party at the palace in Berlin.

My entire crew was invited to the party held on the lawn of the Palace in Berlin. My wife was also invited since she happened to be in Berlin at the time. The sidewalks were lined with spectators, who applauded as we entered the Palace grounds. President Heinemann's daughter spent considerable time with me and my crew so as to practice her English. I might add that she had teenage twin sons who spent time with my wife so that they could practice their English. What a BASH! We had a lovely time and enjoyed ourselves immensely.

The good President, who had written two books while he was Mayor of Cologne, gave me a copy of each. One was published in English and the other in German, and bore his autograph. The flight into Berlin only took about one hour and forty-five minutes. We did not serve meals, but our Stewards or Stewardesses did serve some drinks and refreshments.

One day, while I was burning a few vacation days, I happened to go to the base at Ramstein on an errand. As I neared the Base Exchange or BX, I stopped to allow personnel in a crosswalk to walk across in front of my car. After the crowd had passed, one Airman in fatigue clothing sauntered slowly across the street. When he got right in front of my car, he stopped, stood there yelling at someone on the side of the street, and seemed oblivious to traffic. I was in a hurry, as I beeped my horn at him. He turned and looked at me and started swearing, although I could not decipher his words. He finally cleared the crosswalk, and I pulled over and parked my car. I confronted him, showed him my I.D. Card, and asked to see his. He didn't want to show me his, but I got his name off his uniform. I decided, then and there, that it was, indeed, time for me to retire from the Service. Since discipline was obviously deteriorating, it was time for me to leave. I made the decision to retire six months earlier than I was expected to, and received slightly more pay each month by doing this.

I was given the choice to retire at practically any Air Force Base that I chose, and my choice was Norton AFB, California. This was where my career started its downward drop, and I did have friends who lived in the area, and my children were all at Las Vegas, Nevada, which is close by. The Air Force presented me with a Meritorious Service Medal for my service during the twenty-two years, fifteen days, that I spent in the blue uniform of the USAF. I had definitely wanted to stay in the Air Force for at least thirty years or more, but that was not to be.

CHAPTER XIII
WORKING FOR A LIVING

Following my retirement, I pounded concrete for six solid months before I found a company that would take a chance and hire me. My new boss was Jewish, and an excellent man for whom to work. He put me in charge of a team of men who were rebuilding radio units to be sold back to the Armed Forces. My new place of business was in Los Angeles. I had been turned away from so many companies with the phrase, "You are over-qualified." My new boss was not only good to me, he rewarded my efforts and gave me bonuses from time to time. I supplemented my pay by flying charter flights in small "Bug Smasher" airplanes on very short trips.

About this time, my first daughter, Anne, came to live with me and help me. She got a job as a Legal Secretary, and worked for about one year, in which she was able to buy a car for herself. She then enrolled in Abilene Christian University in Abilene, Texas, to continue her education.

Later, my second daughter, Diana, came to live with me and continue her High School Education. She was going through a very tough time, and finally ran away from home. Six months later, I learned that she was on the East Coast. She later completed her High School work by taking

G.E.D. Examinations, and some college work through the Community College Programs.

I worked with the Electronics Company, who dared to hire me, for two years. Then it was time for me to leave the big city of Los Angeles and return to the land of my birth or the Mid-West. I took a vacation to visit my mother, and while there, I stopped in at my brother's house in Memphis, Tennessee. He drove me around to many of the "Head Hunters" Offices in Memphis, and I finally made contact with the Manager of an Electronics Factory in Smyrna, a suburb of Nashville, Tennessee. Since I was returning to my home in California, this Manager flew over to Memphis to interview me that evening. After the interview, I boarded a flight for the West Coast by way of Dallas, Texas.

After landing at Dallas to change planes, I received a message from Memphis. The brother, who had driven me around that day, had suffered a heart attack at the bowling alley and was dead. I returned to Memphis to remain until after the funeral and burial. While there, I received a call from the Manager who had interviewed me, and was hired.

After these developments, I moved back to Tennessee and started working for Heil-Quaker Electronics Company. I was working as an Electronics Manager, and actually running the plant while my boss was out drumming up business. Then, following this type of work for one to two years, I moved to Murfreesboro, Tennessee, in another company as the Personnel Manager. This job entailed building conveyor belts for Coal Mines. This job lasted for approximately one year, and one day at a football game at Middle Tennessee State University, I ran into the man whom I replaced at the conveyor company.

Jokingly, I mentioned that since he was an Ex-USAF Pilot, and was flying the company plane at his new location, that should he need help with flying it, keep me in mind. About one month later, he phoned me and asked if I was serious about our earlier conversation. I replied, "Most definitely!" He then gave me a date to come to Kentucky for an interview with the President of Pyro Mining Company. Of a surety, I did just that and was hired as the Personnel Manager and spare pilot for the company plane. This plane was a Piper Twin-engine that carried a crew of two and about six passengers. It was not pressurized, and had trouble flying on just one engine with a full passenger load and full fuel tanks. It had to be watched quite carefully.

Since my primary job was the Company Personnel Manager, I discovered that although this company had approximately twelve hundred employees, there was only one company policy on the books. This was absurd, and disaster looking for a place to happen! There were no company rules by which to follow.

However, my boss, who was an Air Force Major General retired, finally got tired of so much flying and the bulk of the trips fell on me. On weekends, I had to fly to various cities and either pick-up or drop-off company VIPs or others who needed help with transportation.

For instance, I was required to fly two of our workers to a place in Wisconsin to obtain information on some equipment that our company had purchased. I advised these two men, who knew absolutely nothing about flying or weather, to expedite their visit because bad weather was expected to be encountered enroute and at our home base. They disregarded my instructions and arrived at the airport later than I had requested. To make a long story short, we flew in weather all the way home, had to be diverted by ground radar around several thunderstorms, and found our home field experiencing rain and thunderstorms. I flew an approach to our field, and encountered turbulence so strong, that I found us upside down over the runway at an altitude of five hundred feet.

How I was able to right the aircraft and make a safe landing, only the LORD knows. Yet, it sent a message to me that I was tired of flying for the company. It didn't break my heart in the least, for I never received one penny for all those weekends and other flights that I made. I was just covered by a large insurance policy, in case I pranged the bird and "bought the farm"; a phrase among fliers meaning, "killed in a crash". The decision was made. I grounded myself and quit flying. With that, my boss also wanted to stop flying, and told me to hire a pilot. I did that on the day after an Air Force Pilot retired from the service. I hung it up, and became a dedicated Ground Pounder.

I then continued to write policies for the company, and conduct an anti-union campaign that resulted in success. We defeated the United Mine Workers in an election, for our pay scales were better than the Union ones. We produced approximately four to five million tons of coal per year. Since I had organized our benefit package, set up a self-insured health package, as well as self-insured life insurance, I asked the President and Chief Financial Officer to allow me fifty cents per ton, and I would set up a retirement plan that would knock the socks off any Union plan. The President and the CFO of the company decided against that and wanted a small Retirement Plan along with a 401K plan. It was obvious why, because they stood to make more money off their ideas, especially with the 401K plan.

CHAPTER XIV
THE ABUNDANT LIFE

During the period of the 1980s, my life took a turn for the better. I can practically describe it as a near miracle, concerning my outlook on life and my religion. I came to learn that I had been incorrectly taught about some religious items during my earlier life, and I had to re-learn some things that I now knew to be absolutely true. I came to know my LORD in a more intimate and spiritual way than before. Then things began to happen to me, and around me, that previously had seemed unreal or untrue.

For instance, I bought a large house in Madisonville, Kentucky, and took quite a few pains to keep house and grounds in tip-top condition at all times. Near the front of the house was a large plant or bush that neither bloomed nor did anything other than to look ratty and scraggly. I hitched my truck to this bush and pulled it out of the ground by the roots. I knew what kind of plant I wanted to replace the bush, something similar to an Irish Juniper. One that grew up more than out. A slender Juniper that would take little horizontal space was the plant that I wanted: but, I couldn't afford to buy one.

Someone quoted some scripture, from the Bible, to me concerning my desire. They said, "Delight yourself also in the LORD, and HE will give you the desires of your heart." Psalm 37: 4. I set out to do just that! I not only tried to keep GOD'S Laws, but also the Local, State, and National Laws as well. I looked around the area in which I lived to see if anyone near me had an Irish Juniper. None were found anywhere in my area. Then one day, about two to three months after removing the bush, I noticed a piece of green, like a small sprig, in the area where the bush had been. I examined it closely and found it to be an Evergreen twig coming up out of the ground. Believe me, it was slender, just like an Irish Juniper, in the exact spot where I wanted it.

Later, I sold the house, but by then, the Juniper had reached the edge of the roof and the last time that I saw it, the top was well above the eave of the house and was almost as high as the peak of the house. And, I had begun to believe that the age of miracles was past. NOT SO!

It fell my duty to assist my daughter and her small child to move from San Diego, California, to Austin, Texas. I loaded my truck with her furniture. It was piled higher than the cab and covered by two tarpaulins. I had a shortage of tie downs for the "tarps", so I supplemented them with Bungee Cords with hooks on each end. Bad move! The Bungees kept working loose, moving about, and allowing wind to get under the tarps. I can't count how many times I stopped to reposition the cords and tighten down the tarps. The second day's driving was really trying to my nerves and patience.

Finally, I reached the top of the Continental Divide, the highest point between the two coasts. I could see for about ten miles in all directions, and I pulled off the road, got out and went around to the right side of my load. I squatted down, reached under the bed to get the loose Bungee Cord, and reattach it to a new location. Suddenly, I noticed two legs standing beside me as I was squatted down. It startled me, to say the least, and I jumped. A man's voice said to me, "I'm sorry, I didn't mean to scare you!

I stood up and faced a man who was standing beside me.

He said, "I have many of those bungee cords in my trunk if you need more."

I thanked him and said, "I don't need more, I just need to reposition the ones that I have,"

I looked at his car that was sitting no more than six feet in front of my truck, yet, I had not heard it drive up or park that close to me. No cars had passed while I was parked off the road. I walked back around my truck and got in. There was no car in front of me or anywhere within miles of me in the Easterly direction. I saw none in the Westerly direction except some very far away. I was, at first, puzzled and then I remembered what the man had said to me, "I'm sorry, I didn't mean to scare you." In the BIBLE, when an Angel appeared to someone, they always began with, "Fear not!" I knew that the church that I attended was praying for my safety while I was on the road alone, and a miracle had just been performed for my benefit.

One night, after I had gone to sleep, I was awakened by my wife.

She said, "Jim, there is someone in the bedroom with us." I raised up, looked around, saw nothing, and said, "Go back to sleep, Babe. You must have had a bad dream."

She replied, "But Jim, I haven't been asleep yet." He's standing at the foot of the bed, can't you see him?"

I looked again, saw nothing, and remembered that I had locked up and set the Burglar Alarm prior to coming to bed. I turned over and quickly fell asleep again.

The next morning, I asked her to tell me about her dream. Again, she replied that she had not been asleep, and it was no dream! I queried her further, and she told me what happened. Apparently, she had not heard anything, she just sensed someone in the room with us. Then she saw a very large, tall man standing at the foot of the bed. That's when she awakened me. I asked her if he said anything.

She said, "No, he didn't speak, but just smiled at me." Then he came around to her side of the bed, reached down with his hand, and touched her left shoulder.

My wife had experienced a frozen right shoulder, and had it corrected and broken loose while under anesthesia. This is a very painful procedure. At this time, her left shoulder was frozen or locked up, and we had scheduled another surgical procedure. After the being, which most assuredly was an angel, touched her left shoulder, it was as free as a bird!

She said, "Look", and she put her shoulder and arm through all kinds of movements and exercises. Later, she always referred to the healing done by "Her Angel" as sent from GOD. Who would argue the point with her?" I think that he did show up on one more occasion, as my Dear Wife lay dying.

It should be obvious to the reader of this book that my survival through all these scrapes and bangs is somewhat unusual to say the least. Some might think that I lived a charmed life. Not so! Our LORD kept me alive for his purposes, not mine. And I truly believe that HE poured out his wonderful grace for a reason. Furthermore, I believe

I would be remiss if I didn't give HIM praise and glory for HIS goodness and mercy. As we advance in age, and begin to look back in retrospect, it is then that we recognize that GOD has had HIS hand on us for many years, and in ways unrecognizable at the time of occurrence. This age in which we live, the age of grace, is as real as rain!

I'm going to list a few things that occurred in my lifetime to exemplify how GOD'S GRACE has kept me alive.

At five years of age, I was held on the ground by a cow that was trying to gore me. My sister-in-law ran the cow away with a hoe.

At six years of age, my brother ran over me with our car. No bones broken, just bruises and contusions.

At nine years of age, I helped one of my older brothers load firewood on an old truck that had its cab removed. After loading, we went lickety-split down through the woods and hit a tree. I was thrown off and the wood piled on top of me. Only bruises and contusions.

At age ten, I had not learned to swim and almost drowned myself and my sister in a lake. We were both rescued and both survived.

At age sixteen, while traveling to a high school basketball game in a pick-up truck with four other teenagers, we flipped over and rolled into a deep ditch. I received a knot on my head, but went on to the game and played in it. It was one of my better performances.

At age seventeen, while swimming in a creek, my foot slipped as I dived from a thirty-foot high bank into the water. Realizing that I was about to hit in shallow water, I rolled up into a ball while turning my head off to one side. I hit the shallow bottom, fracturing my left collarbone. No broken neck!

Then came my military career. I was assigned a position as Detachment Commander of a unit at Point Barrow, Alaska. I was caught twice in a "white out", and had to be rescued after sitting all night in my vehicle with the engine and heater going. Outside temperature was approximately thirty degrees below zero.

Also, at Point Barrow, a drunken Eskimo jabbed me several times in the belly with an eighteen inch skinning knife. Two other Eskimo men, who were walking by, saw what was happening, ran up and held the attacker until I could get in my vehicle and leave.

While flying from Japan to the Island of Guam, we encountered weather almost the whole way. Unknown to us at the time, we were flying through the middle of a typhoon that we neither expected nor was forecast. We survived.

Once, over the North Atlantic Ocean, at night, and in rough weather conditions, while enroute from Scotland to the United States, we experienced an engine failure and were required to divert to Iceland. The weather there was at minimums for any aircraft, but we landed safely and were very happy to be on the ground.

Another flight from Dallas to our home base in California, resulted in an emergency landing at Cedar City, Utah, after experiencing the failure of two engines on the same wing. No problem.

Flying for many years, one finds many things that can, and do, occur that create a bit of concern for one's safety and longevity! I have encountered thunderstorms when they were not expected over Italy, the Pyrenees Mountains between France and Spain, and in a small corridor that we were required to remain in, while flying to and from Berlin, Germany.

In 1961, while living in Southern California, I was involved in an auto accident wherein I suffered a broken neck, broken thumb, fractured ribs, and numerous bruises and lacerations.

While flying the company plane in 1981, I found myself up-side down over the Sturgis, Kentucky, airport at five hundred feet altitude, under the effects of a thunderstorm. The landing was made safely with no injuries or damage to the airplane.

In 1982, while driving to work very early one morning, I attempted to pass a vehicle just before daylight. Suddenly, I saw a vehicle coming toward me without lights and in my lane. I swerved to avoid the head on collision, lost control of my vehicle, went off the road, across a ditch, which tore off both of my rear wheels. I sustained a broken back, bruises and lacerations. Hospitalization was required.

In 1991, while mowing my yard with a riding lawn mower, the mower flipped over backwards on top of me, fracturing my left shoulder.

Finally, in 1994, following a Cursillo Retreat weekend, I suffered a Heart Attack. It seemed that whenever I tried to do some work for the LORD, I noticed resistance directed toward me. Why then, have I listed all these close shaves and times when I looked Death in the face? Because, these are irrefutable proof to me of GOD'S grace, mercy and protection.

This is, most definitely, the AGE OF GRACE. The last stage before the return of our LORD JESUS CHRIST. It would behoove us to always remember this fact, and keep our minds and hearts tuned to obey our LORD AND SAVIOR and expect HIS RETURN more sooner than later.

EPILOGUE

The author of this tale was able to reach some of the goals that he had set for himself, and was the receiver of much satisfaction in so doing. Self-confidence comes from setting goals and achieving them. It is a rare thing when someone reaches all of the goals that were set at an earlier date: however, an earnest effort usually produces desired results or very nearly reaches the goal. The object of this book is to encourage young men and women to first, set the goals that are commensurate with your desires, and second, pursue the ends desired with all of your effort, strength and mind. Do not allow anyone to discourage you or attempt to convince you to abandon your goals. Remember, that it is by the grace of our creator that we succeed at anything that we attempt. It is the work of the "enemy" that tries to sidetrack or derail us into frustration, disgust, and failure, for although very good at deception and evil, he is a failure at being the "covering cherub" and a powerful angel. He is a liar, the father of lies, and comes only to steal, kill, and destroy.

Without GOD in our lives, a dependence upon HIM, and determination to reach our goals, it will be rare if we really do reach and attain any goals that we have set. Very rarely, will we be aware of what GOD has planned for us, but we can easily see HIS mighty hand at work in our lives, and by putting HIM first, all these other things will be given to us as well. May GOD bless you, my friend.

About the Author

Jim Shouse was born in Prentiss County, Mississippi, the youngest of eleven children. His parents, highly regarded throughout the area in which he grew up, were strong devout Christians. His younger years were spent in rural America; he attended High School in Wheeler, Mississippi, and Community College in Booneville, Mississippi. He is a graduate of the University of Nebraska at Omaha, and did graduate work at Southern Illinois University, Edwardsville, Illinois. He served twenty-two years as Pilot, Navigator, and Observer in the United States Air Force, retiring as a Lieutenant Colonel. His last assignment, accomplished in West Germany during the Cold War, was especially fulfilling. As Aircraft Commander of USAF multiengine aircraft, his passengers included: the President of West Germany, Gustav Heinemann and his governmental team, the Chancellor of West Germany, Willie Brandt, the Commander of the United States Air Forces Europe and later Chairman of the Joint Chiefs of Staff, David Jones, the Commander of the Strategic Air Command, General Dougherty, and numerous Senators, Congressmen and Congresswomen, and other Very Important Persons.

He is the father of one son and three daughters, and makes his home in Morganfield, Kentucky. As a retiree from the USAF, a local business, and Spoken Word Ministries, wherein he performed six biblical characters in First Person Narrative throughout eleven different states, he now devotes himself to speaking engagements and serving our DEAR LORD.